WEAVING
HAND TOWELS
SIMPLY

WEAVING
HAND TOWELS
SIMPLY

43 DESIGNS FOR
4- AND 8-SHAFT LOOMS

SUSAN KESLER-SIMPSON

STACKPOLE
BOOKS
Essex, Connecticut
Blue Ridge Summit, Pennsylvania

STACKPOLE BOOKS

An imprint of Globe Pequot, the trade division of The
Rowman & Littlefield Publishing Group, Inc.
4501 Forbes Blvd., Ste. 200
Lanham, MD 20706
www.rowman.com

Distributed by NATIONAL BOOK NETWORK
800-462-6420

British Library Cataloguing in Publication Information
available

Library of Congress Cataloging-in-Publication Data
Names: Kesler-Simpson, Susan, author.
Title: Weaving hand towels simply : 43 designs for 4- and
  8-shaft looms / Susan Kesler-Simpson.
Description: First edition. | Essex, Connecticut : Stackpole
  Books, 2024. | Summary: "This collection of hand towel
  patterns is just the reference you need! With 43 designs in a
  variety of weave structures, from easy to advanced patterns,
  for both 4- and 8-shaft looms, there are plenty of patterns to
  explore and learn from while you make practical towels"—
  Provided by publisher.
Identifiers: LCCN 2023055858 (print) | LCCN 2023055859
  (ebook) | ISBN 9780811772860 (paperback) | ISBN
  9780811772877 (epub)
Subjects: LCSH: Hand weaving. | Hand weaving—Patterns.
Classification: LCC TT848 .K478 2024 (print) | LCC TT848
  (ebook) | DDC 746.9/8—dc23/eng/20240109
LC record available at https://lccn.loc.gov/2023055858
LC ebook record available at https://lccn.loc.gov/2023055859

™ The paper used in this publication meets the minimum
requirements of American National Standard for Information
Sciences—Permanence of Paper for Printed Library Materials,
ANSI/NISO Z39.48-1992.

First Edition

CONTENTS

TOWELS

INTRODUCTION

Hand towels and dish towels are a staple of the weaver's life. Many years ago, I thought weaving towels was a rather odd thing to do since they were so easily available and inexpensive at the store. Then a group I belonged to decided to have a towel exchange. I wove my requisite towels, and I was hooked! Hand-woven towels are an expression of creativity and love. They are small projects that can be easily finished and allow weavers to express themselves. These small projects are wonderful canvases on which to try new colors and weaving styles.

It is always a wonderful idea to have a dozen or so towels set aside. They are perfect for wrapping a casserole you are taking to someone who is ill. Towels are the ideal housewarming gift when woven in the recipient's colors. Do you know someone who is having a new baby? Normally you would not think of towels, but why not? Instead of calling it a hand towel or dish towel, call your creation a burping cloth! A new parent can never have enough of those. While you are weaving, you might also think about weaving a matching blanket.

Recently, a friend's husband had a serious farm accident. Karen had woven a number of towels for Christmas gifts. But as her friends came to weed the flower beds, help her catch up on laundry, and bring them meals, she was happy to send each of those friends on their way with a beautiful hand-woven towel to say "thank you."

Towels do not have to be just for the kitchen. A lovely hand-woven towel in a guest bathroom can make such a statement. And these towels can be a bit fancier than ones we would use in the kitchen.

So, whether you are a person who dresses your loom for two towels or the one who puts on a 10-yard warp to make many, many towels, we all know that hand towels are here to stay. The warps for the projects in this book are for two towels. The width measurements given indicate the width on the loom! This is an important number to know to be able to center the warp. Remember that your towel will be narrower after finishing. If you prefer wider towels, it is easy to add repeats or borders. My preference is for smaller towels, so keep this point in mind as you look at the instructions and plan your towels. The instructions will tell you how many repeats or the length to weave each towel. To weave more than the two in the project, just add another 30 inches (76.2 cm) for each towel. I hope that you enjoy weaving these towels as much as I did creating them.

Back to Basics

A complete weaving draft can be overwhelming for the new weaver. Even as we get more experience, there are small things that crop up that can be confusing. So, let's begin at the beginning. Figure 1.1 shows a simple and complete weaving graph for a 4-shaft loom. There are four components to this graph:

1. Threading
2. Treadling
3. Tie-up
4. Drawdown

Threading

We will begin by looking at the threading chart (Figure 1.2).

Threading charts are read from the right to the left. The numbers in the blocks indicate the number of the shaft, not the number of threads.

In some of the older drafts, you will not see the number of the shaft indicated. In *A Handweaver's Pattern Book* (Davison), for example, you will see the threading indicated with lines. The 4-shaft threading in Figure 1.2 would look like it does in Figure 1.3.

Threading

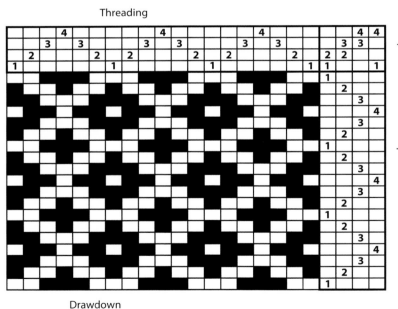

Tie-up

Treadling

Drawdown

Figure 1.1. Simple 4-shaft weaving draft.

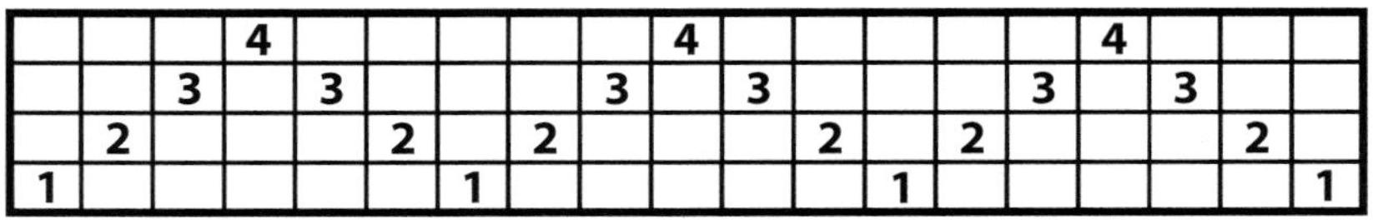

Figure 1.2. Threading chart.

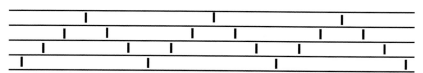

Figure 1.3. Threading chart with lines indicating shafts.

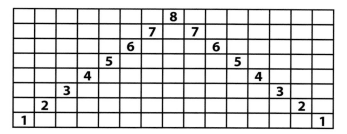
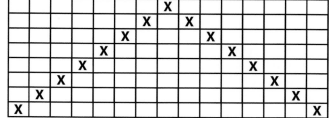

Figure 1.4. Threading examples for an 8-shaft loom.

Compare the two threading charts. They mean exactly the same thing, just in a different style.

Figure 1.4 shows the threading for an 8-shaft loom in both styles. Once again, there is only one thread per block. In the chart to the left, the number indicates only the number of the shaft.

Next, we will look at another situation that can confuse weavers. Threading drafts can be very long, so weavers/authors often use brackets to reduce the size. Look at the threading chart below, and you will see a different method of writing a threading chart.

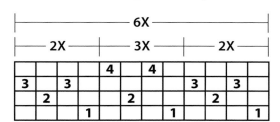

Figure 1.5. A shorter way to chart long threading drafts.

Look at the first threading block (Figure 1.6):

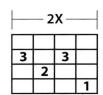

Figure 1.6. The first threading block.

Above this block you see the brackets, and inside the brackets you see "2X." This means that this portion of the chart is repeated two times. If it were written out fully, it would look like this (Figure 1.7):

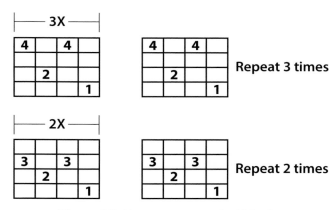

Figure 1.7. All repeats charted.

Looking again at the chart in Figure 1.5, you will see two more blocks that are repeated in the same manner (Figure 1.8).

Figure 1.8. Two more repeated blocks.

So, instead of having this long threading draft with seven blocks written out, you just have the three blocks. This is just a shorter way of indicating the total of 28 ends.

Look again at Figure 1.5, and you will see there is another bracket *above the entire chart*! This means that you will repeat the entire sequence six times. Earlier, you found that the sequence was a total of 28 ends. Since this is repeated six times, your total for this draft is 6 × 28 = 168 ends.

Using brackets is very common in books. Always start with the brackets closest to the draft and work out from there. You may also see brackets such as these in treadling drafts. Just follow the same procedure. Remember, if it gets too confusing when threading the loom or treadling, just write the draft out in full either on graph paper or using your computer software and work from that.

Treadling

Next, we will look at the treadling portion of the weaving chart (Figure 1.9).

Treadling charts are vertical and generally to the right of the drawdown. In Figure 1.9, the number indicates the treadle that is to be used. You will also see treadling charts written with X's instead of numbers, as in Figure 1.10.

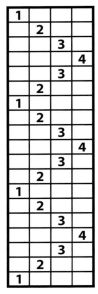

Figure 1.9. Treadling draft.

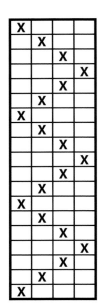

Figure 1.10. Treadling draft with X's instead of numbers.

You may also see brackets along the side of the treadling graph, just as seen in the examples of the threading with brackets. Always start with the information in the bracket closest to the chart and work out from there. And remember, you can write out the treadling chart in full if that is easier for you.

Another example of a treadling chart using both lines and numbers as seen in *A Handweaver's Pattern Book* is shown in Figure 1.11.

In Figure 1.11, there are no blocks—just the vertical lines. The small, single lines indicate one repeat of that treadle. On treadle 1 you see a "4," which means to repeat treadle 1, four times. This is common with overshot and summer and winter weaves.

Do you read/treadle the chart from the top to bottom or bottom to top? Always read your book/pattern carefully, because you may see that the author is asking you to read/weave the chart from the *bottom up*. This is often indicated by an arrow along the edge of the chart, as seen in Figure 1.12.

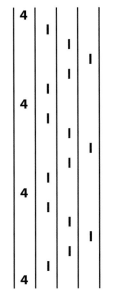

Figure 1.11. An example of a chart using both lines and numbers.

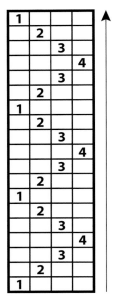

Figure 1.12. An arrow is sometimes included to indicate the direction to read the chart.

Many times whether you work top to bottom or bottom to top makes no difference, but I want you to understand why bottom to top makes sense. Think about the orientation of your loom as compared to the chart in Figure 1.11. Start at the bottom, and weave the first thread on treadle 1. When you weave the second thread on treadle 2, you are laying that thread right above the first thread (Figure 1.13).

The threads are being woven in exactly as the chart is written. Reading from the top down is just the reverse

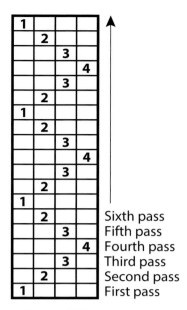

Sixth pass
Fifth pass
Fourth pass
Third pass
Second pass
First pass

Figure 1.13.

as the threads are being woven in. A computer software program is a great way to check to see whether it will make a difference weaving top to bottom or bottom to top. Failing to check on this point may result in your pattern not looking as you had wished.

In summer and winter patterns, there are often images such as cats or ghosts. These are directional motifs. In one location you may read the treadling from the top down and then in another location read the treadling from the bottom up.

Tie-up

This small portion of the graph tells you how your treadles are to be tied to the shafts. The chart in Figure 1.1, shown again below in Figure 1.14, is for a 4-shaft loom.

		4	4
	3	3	
2	2		
1			1

Figure 1.14. Sample tie-up for a 4-shaft loom.

Let's break this down to each component.

In Figure 1.15, note that the first column is highlighted. The numbers in this column mean that the treadle 1 will be connected to both shaft 1 and shaft 2. If you have a loom where the treadles are already connected to the shafts and cannot be changed, you will use both feet and depress the treadles that are

connected to shaft 1 and shaft 2 together. This is called a direct tie-up loom.

		4	4
	3	3	
2	2		
1			1

Figure 1.15. Treadle 1 will be connected to shafts 1 and 2.

In Figure 1.16, the second column is highlighted.

		4	4
	3	3	
2	2		
1			1

Figure 1.16. Treadle 2 will be connected to shafts 2 and 3.

This means that treadle 2 will be connected to both shaft 2 and shaft 3. If you have a direct tie-up loom, you will use both feet and depress the treadles that are connected to shaft 2 and shaft 3 together.

In Figure 1.17, the third column is highlighted.

		4	4
	3	3	
2	2		
1			1

Figure 1.17. Treadle 3 will be connected to shafts 3 and 4.

This means that treadle 3 will be connected to both shaft 3 and shaft 4. If you have a direct tie-up loom, you will use both feet and depress the treadles that are connected to shaft 3 and shaft 4 together.

In Figure 1.18, the fourth column is highlighted.

		4	4
	3	3	
2	2		
1			1

Figure 1.18. Treadle 4 will be connected to shafts 1 and 4.

This means that treadle 4 will be connected to both shaft 1 and shaft 4. And if you have a direct tie-up loom, you will use both feet and depress the treadles that are connected to shaft 1 and 4.

For an 8-shaft loom, you might see multiple shafts tied to one treadle. It all depends on what weave structure you are weaving.

There is one more thing that you need to understand with tie-up charts. You need to know what type of loom you are working with. All of my charts/patterns are for a jack loom. With a jack loom, when you depress the treadles, the shafts are *raised*! If you have a countermarch loom, when you depress the treadles, your shafts will be *lowered*. It is very important that you know this when you are dressing your loom. If you have a jack loom and the tie-up is for a countermarch, your design will be on the underneath side. That really isn't a problem except that we like to see the pattern emerge as we weave. There is a way to fix this issue. Look at Figure 1.19:

Figure 1.19. Tie-up for the same pattern on jack loom and countermarch loom.

Both of these tie-ups would result in the same pattern. Notice the difference! When the jack loom uses shafts 1 and 2, the countermarch uses shafts 3 and 4. Jack loom: 2 and 3; countermarch loom: 1 and 4. If you look closely, you will see that every empty square in the tie-up for the jack loom is filled in for the countermarch loom. If you have a jack loom and the pattern is for a countermarch, just change the tie-up as indicated here. *A Handweaver's Pattern Book* by Davison is written for a countermarch loom. Any time I use one of those patterns, I change the tie-up to one for a jack loom.

Multi-pedal Treadling

This is a term that you will see and need to use on occasion, so I want to explain what it is and why it is used. First, let's go back to the 4-shaft loom tie-up (Figure 1.20).

We know that when you depress treadle 1, it raises shafts 1 and 2. But there are 4-shaft looms that are *direct tie-up*. These looms have only four treadles, and each treadle is tied to one shaft. This cannot be changed! So,

Figure 1.20. Sample tie-up for a 4-shaft loom.

				T	T
		4	4		4
	3	3		3	
2	2				
1			1	1	

Figure 1.20. Sample tie-up for a 4-shaft loom.

if you look at the tie-up in Figure 1.20, how would you treadle it? You would use both of your feet and step on treadle 1 and treadle 2, raising both simultaneously. This is multi-pedal treadling for a 4-shaft loom. To raise shafts 2 and 3, you would step on both treadles to raise those simultaneously, and so on. I included a tabby with this tie-up so you can see that to get a tabby, you would use treadles 1 and 3. Once you get used to using both feet, it is really very easy.

Now on to the 8-shaft loom. We are working with many more shafts, so you will always be able to tie up the treadles as needed. There are no direct tie-up 8-shaft looms. But there are still times when you will have to do multi-pedal treadling. Look at Figure 1.21. This is the tie-up and treadling for the All about Cats towels.

								T	T
8	8					8			8
							7		7
					6				6
				5	5		5		5
4	4			4	4	4	4		4
3	3	3	3	3	3	3	3		3
	2		2		2			2	
1		1		1				1	
			X						
				X					
					X		X		
					X		X		
				X			X		
X							X		
	X						X		
X							X		
	X						X		
X							X		
	X						X		
X									
	X								
		X							
			X						
		X							
			X						
		X							
			X						
		X							
	X								
X									
	X						X		
X									
	X								
X									
	X								
X									
			X			X			
		X				X			

Figure 1.21. Tie-up and treadling for All about Cats.

Working top to bottom, this treadling begins with treadle 5 and then treadle 6. Then we begin to do multi-pedal treadling. The next line includes both treadles 6 and 8, the next one 5 and 8. Look through the complete treadling, and you will see a number of places where you will use both feet and depress two treadles simultaneously to raise the proper shafts. It is necessary to depress both treadles to create the motif.

When I was designing the cats, the original tie-up included the 8 shafts *but with 14 treadles!* That certainly wasn't going to work! There is a fantastic free online program to help when this issue happens. It is called Tim's Treadle Reducer, and this program creates what is called a skeleton tie-up. It reduces the number of treadles by combining them in a manner that works for your design but results in the need for multi-pedal treadling. This program is very easy to use. You put in the number of shafts, the number of treadles your design is using, and the number of treadles you have available. Then submit! The results will come back almost immediately. But do be aware that there are times when it just can't be done. That is always disappointing, but just return to your original design and make some changes and then try again.

Drawdown

Finally, we want to look at the drawdown portion of the chart. The drawdown is a visual image of what your weaving project will look like.

Looking at Figure 1.22, it is very easy to see the design! There are black diamonds and crosses on a white background. The drawdown shows the final result of the interaction of the threading, tie-up, and treadling. Whew, that was a mouthful! So how does that work?

I'm just going to use the first four treadlings of this pattern for the explanation. We will begin by looking at Figure 1.23. The explanation will be referring to a jack loom.

In the example, the number 1 treadle has been highlighted in red. Treadle 1 raises shafts 1 and 2, which are highlighted in blue in the tie-up. Next, I highlighted every "1" and "2" in the threading in green. Now you have to put a visual thinking cap on. When you depress treadle 1, it *raises* shafts 1 and 2, so every thread in the threading draft that is on shafts 1 and 2 are raised. This means that when you throw your shuttle, your black weft thread will go *under* these warp threads (highlighted in cream) and will go over all of the threads on shafts 3 and 4.

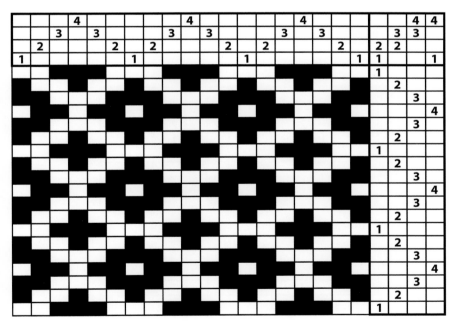

Figure 1.22.
Drawdown.

Figure 1.23.

On to the next line. In Figure 1.24, the number 2 treadle has been highlighted in red. Treadle 2 raises shafts 2 and 3, which are highlighted in blue in the tie-up. Next, I highlighted every "2" and "3" in the threading in green. Put that visual thinking cap on again! When you depress treadle 2, it *raises* shafts 2 and 3, so every thread in the threading draft that is on shafts 2 and 3 is raised. This means that when you throw your shuttle, your black weft thread will go *under* these warp threads (which are highlighted in cream) and will go over all of the threads on shafts 1 and 4.

On to the next line. In Figure 1.25, the number 3 treadle is highlighted in red. Treadle 3 raises shafts 3 and 4, highlighted in blue. Every thread on 3 and 4 in the threading draft is indicated in green. When you depress treadle 3, all of the threads on shafts 3 and 4

are raised. When you throw your weft thread, which is black, it will go under these threads and over every thread on shafts 1 and 2.

And, finally, we come to the last line. In Figure 1.26, treadle 4 is highlighted in red. Treadle 4 raises shafts 1 and 4, highlighted in blue. Every thread on 1 and 4 in the threading is highlighted in green. When you depress treadle 4, all of the threads on shafts 1 and 4 are raised. Your weft thread, which is black, will go under these threads and over all threads on shafts 2 and 3, which are highlighted in cream.

This can be a hard concept to understand, so don't get frustrated. Just go over it slowly, and soon you will see how all of the components are connected.

We have now covered the basic draft and all of its components.

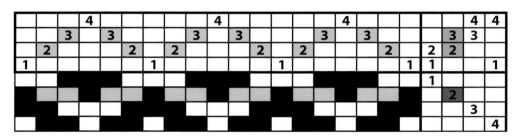

Figure 1.24.

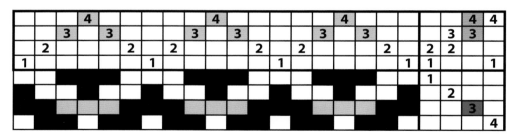

Figure 1.25.

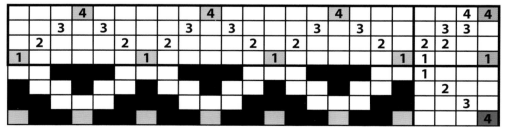

Figure 1.26.

2 Profile Drafts

Profile Threading

This is another term and technique that is used in weaving that causes much confusion. Weavers/authors use a profile draft as a space-saving technique and as a design technique. Beginning with the basics, we will first look at how a profile draft saves space.

In Figure 2.1, you will see a simple profile draft shown in two different ways. They both say the same thing.

Figure 2.1. Sample profile draft.

Remember, this is not a threading draft—the rows do not correspond to shafts! And this chart is incomplete! There are various traditional weave structures that have specific patterns for their threading blocks. These blocks always remain the same and are unchanging. Summer

and winter is one of those weave structures. Figure 2.2 shows the two threading blocks for summer and winter for a 4-shaft loom.

Looking at the profile draft, where you see the letter A, you will substitute the four-thread Block A. Where you see the letter B, you will substitute the four-thread Block B. Figure 2.3 shows this relationship.

In this example, the top of the graph shows Blocks A and B. The red arrows start at Block A and point to every A in the profile draft. The black arrows start at Block B and point to every B in the graph. Now to the final step! In Figure 2.4, the four-thread blocks have been substituted for every lettered block.

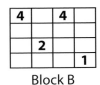
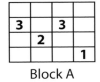

Figure 2.2. The two threading blocks for summer and winter on a 4-shaft loom.

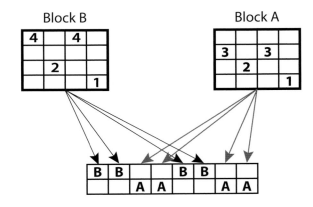

Figure 2.3.

Figure 2.4.

Notice the difference in the size of the threading graph! Compare Figures 2.1 and 2.4. They look very different, but both graphs say the same thing! This method allows you to present a long threading draft in a shorter manner.

Look at the following two blocks in Figure 2.5. We have made two twill blocks for this example.

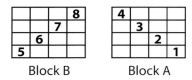

Figure 2.5. Two twill blocks.

If you substitute these blocks into the same profile draft in Figure 2.1, Figure 2.6 shows the complete threading.

But now we have gone from a 4-shaft design in Figure 2.4 to an 8-shaft design in Figure 2.6. *The weave structure you have chosen to substitute into the profile draft will determine the number of shafts needed.*

In these examples, we had only Block A and Block B. You will find other charts that have more blocks. Let's look at one! In Figure 2.7, you will see a profile draft with four different blocks.

I will keep this profile draft short so you will be able to see the final threading chart in full. In this next exercise, we will be looking at the four threading blocks associated with the weave structure known as Quigley. These blocks are shown in Figure 2.8.

The substitution process is the same. In Figure 2.9, you will see arrows from the Quigley Blocks to the blocks in the profile draft.

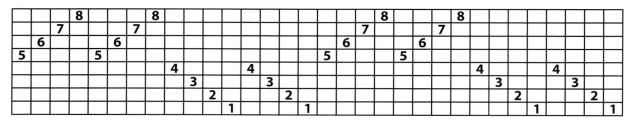

Figure 2.6.

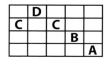

Figure 2.7. Four blocks for a profile draft.

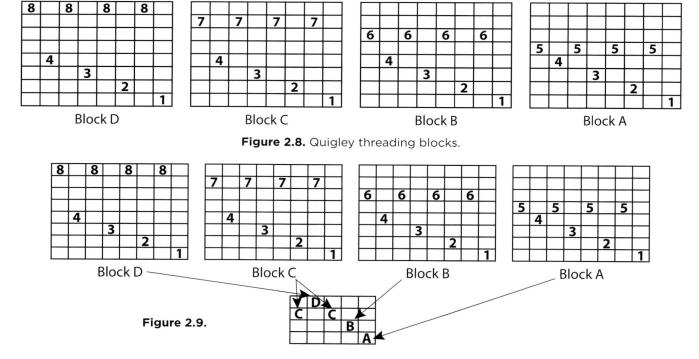

Figure 2.8. Quigley threading blocks.

Figure 2.9.

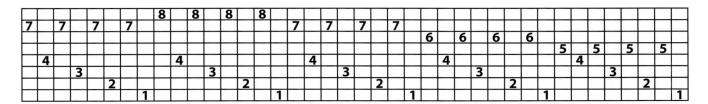

Figure 2.10.

Figure 2.10 shows this threading chart in full.

Profile drafts are a convenient way to communicate the information for threading in a compact form.

Now we will move ahead to profile treadling!

Profile Treadling

Is there such a thing as profile drafts for treadling? Of course! Often with various weave patterns there are specific treadling patterns. Let's begin with summer and winter. There are four basic treadling patterns associated with summer and winter. Figure 2.11 shows them written out in full.

In the draft shown in Figure 2.12, the treadling pattern blocks have been indicated in red and also with letters. Remember, this is *a profile treadling pattern!*

Your choice of treadling pattern from Figure 2.11 is then substituted for each red square in Figure 2.12. So that there is no question, I have written out the first three blocks of the treadling graph using treadling Pattern 1/Pairs "O"s in Figure 2.13.

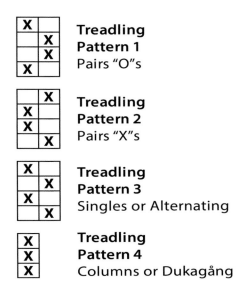

Treadling Pattern 1
Pairs "O"s

Treadling Pattern 2
Pairs "X"s

Treadling Pattern 3
Singles or Alternating

Treadling Pattern 4
Columns or Dukagång

Figure 2.11. Four basic treadling patterns of summer and winter.

ANY of the treadling pattern blocks can be substituted for each red square. It makes no difference if you

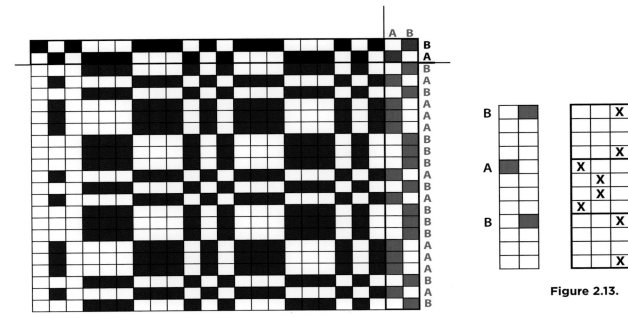

Figure 2.12.

Figure 2.13.

are doing four shafts or more. Choose one treadling method and substitute the appropriate threads for one red block. Or you might use a mixture of the treadling methods. In the case of patterns 3 or 4, you can repeat the treadles as desired. A note here: In my projects, the drafts do not use profile treadling. Each block is written in full so that you know exactly which method I used. If you remember from Figure 2.11, your choice of treadling methods will change the final look of your project. Feel free to change the method if you wish for your project, but know that it will change the look. A computer drafting program is a great tool for help with this step, both for visualizing your pattern and for documenting your plan.

There are other weave structures that have specific treadling patterns. Unlike summer and winter, there is less flexibility in the treadling. Once again, they will be indicated by blocks or letters, as in Figure 2.1. Look at

Figure 2.14, which shows two profile treadling charts that both say the same thing. The substitution process is just the same as in the threading profile.

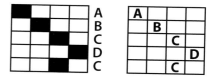

Figure 2.14. These two profile treadling charts both mean the same thing.

In the next exercise, we will use the treadling for the Quigley weave structure. Figure 2.15 shows the four treadling blocks associated with Quigley. Note that this is a multi-pedal treadling.

In Figure 2.16, you will see the arrows from the Quigley treadling block to the correct block in the profile chart.

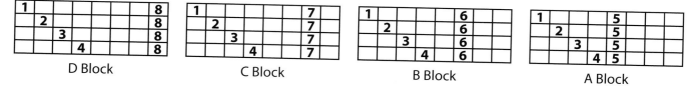

Figure 2.15. Quigley treadling blocks.

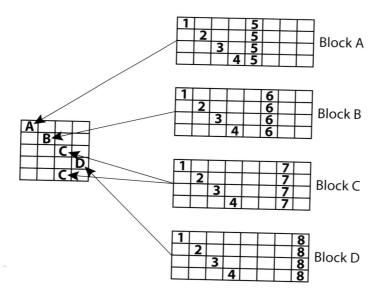

Figure 2.16.

In Figure 2.17, the treadling chart is complete.

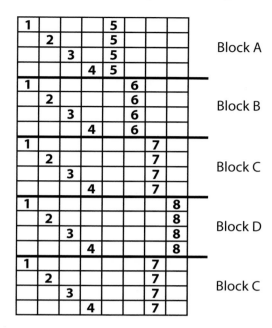

Figure 2.17.

(Block labels, top to bottom: Block A, Block B, Block C, Block D, Block C)

Tie-up

We have looked at profile threading and profile treadling. What about the tie-up? The tie-up will depend on the weave structure. It will be different for summer and winter, Quigley, or twill. A profile tie-up is unusual, but it is possible to find one. *A Weaver's Book of 8-Shaft Patterns* by Strickler uses profile tie-ups in the section on summer and winter. We will look at just one (Figure 2.18).

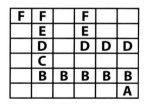

Figure 2.18. Profile tie-up.

Looking at Figure 2.18 as is makes absolutely no sense. But there are full tie-ups included in the text. Sometimes they are beside the profile draft, but know that they will be on the page. It is important that you have some familiarity with summer and winter to fully understand the tie-up. But—moving forward—the full threading in the Strickler book is written out as in Figure 2.19.

		F	F			F	F					D	D
		E	E			E	E					D	D
		D	D			D	D					B	B
		C	C			D	D	D	D			B	A
a	**b**	**F**	**F**	**B**	**B**	**B**	**B**	**B**	**B**	**B**	**B**	**A**	**A**
	o					o	o			o	o	o	o
	o	o	o			o	o			o	o	o	o
	o	o	o			o	o						
	o	o	o			o	o						
	o	o	o			o	o	o	o	o	o	o	o
	o	o	o	o	o	o	o	o	o	o			
o		o		o		o		o		o			o
o	o		o		o		o		o		o		

Figure 2.19.

The "a" and "b" indicate your tabby tie-up shafts. If you compare Figures 2.18 and 2.19, they mean the same thing, but Figure 2.19 is the *full* tie-up. The difference in the tie-ups with the same letter is the use of either shaft 1 *or* shaft 2. This is a consistent feature in all summer and winter treadling. Look at Figure 2.20. Shafts 3 through 7 are used for both treadles. The only difference is one column includes shaft 1 and the other column includes shaft 2.

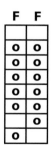

Figure 2.20.

Look again at Figure 2.19, and you will immediately realize that an 8-shaft loom has only 10 treadles and this tie-up uses 14 treadles. Not to worry! Remember that earlier I told you about Tim's Treadle Reducer. Put this chart into the program, and it will reduce to a usable tie-up if possible. Then you will need to adjust the treadling pattern, and you will also be multi-pedal treadling. This is where a computer program is a huge help. You can put all the information into your program and verify that you have made all the changes correctly.

Profile Drafts as a Design Tool

Profile drafts are also used as a designing tool. Again, it is a shorthand method to see how the design might look in a basic form. Blocks are filled in and a chart is formed. See Figure 2.21.

This chart shows you a *design*! Whatever weave structure you choose to use and substitute into the blocks will result in this basic design. You could use summer and winter, Bergman, or Quigley. It is much easier and faster to design an overall pattern in this method and *then*, once you have decided that you like the look, go back and substitute the full threading blocks and the appropriate tie-up.

Let's look at how this process works. In Figure 2.22, I have highlighted a section of the profile design in red. This is the section we will work with.

In Figure 2.23, I have substituted a summer and winter threading and treadling with the appropriate tie-up. Compare Figure 2.23 to the red square in Figure 2.22. The light-colored X-shaped pattern is visible in both.

Remember, you could substitute Bergman, Quigley, or twill into the same profile design, and looking at Figure 2.21, you already have an idea what your final design will look like. Designing in this manner is a fast and easy way to determine whether you like the overall look before going to the work of putting in all the threading and treadling.

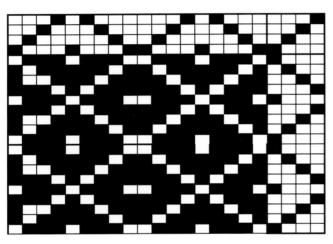

Figure 2.21.

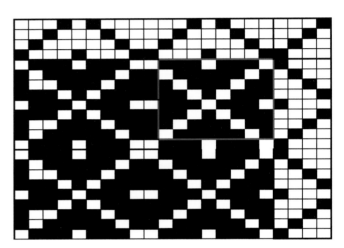

Figure 2.22.

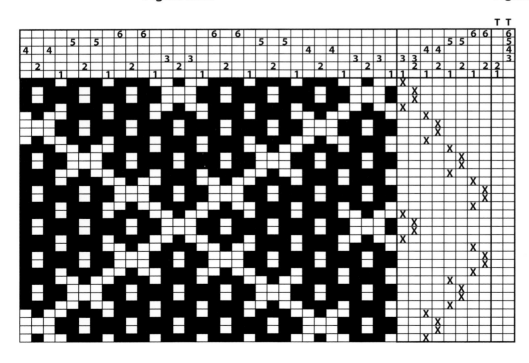

Figure 2.23.

Computer Programs

Oh, those computer programs! They are wonderful to have and use. They allow us to design patterns quickly, make changes, and add color and size of thread. But they are not perfect! Squares become rectangles; circles become ovals—definitely not what we thought they would look like. And sometimes we are very disappointed.

What You See Is Not Always What You Get

This is the biggest problem with a computer program.

If you can weave a perfect balanced weave, you will get something like the image in Figure 3.1. But that can be hard to do. If your beat is not hard enough, the lovely diamonds become elongated (Figure 3.2).

But if you beat too hard, your diamonds are squished (Figure 3.3)!

Not only can the beat affect the shape of the diamonds, but let's assume that you are using 10/2 cotton for the warp and decide to use 8/2 or 5/2 cotton for the weft. Since those threads are thicker, you will once again elongate your diamonds. If getting a perfect diamond is your goal, then it is important that you sample before you start your final project. Factor in the size of your warp and weft threads. You may have to adjust your sett also. Increasing from 12 to 14 will allow the

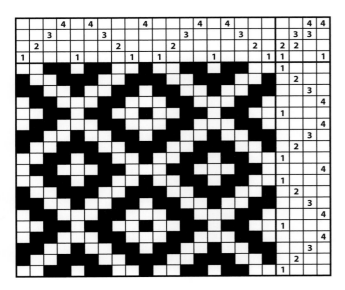

Figure 3.1. Balanced weave with perfect beat.

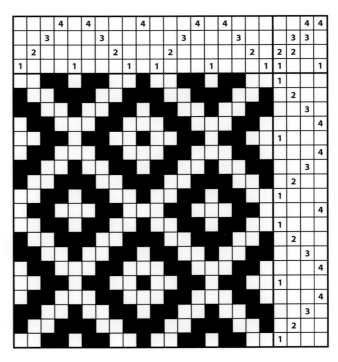

Figure 3.2. Diamonds are elongated because the beat was not firm enough.

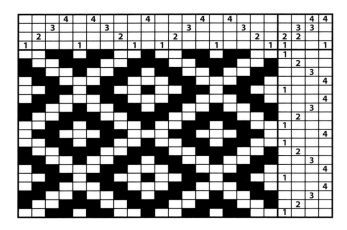

Figure 3.3. If your beat is too hard, your diamonds will be squished.

weft threads to beat in more easily. Or decreasing from 12 to 10 will make it harder to beat in the weft thread.

Let's look at an overshot draft that has a beautiful motif. Overshot is one of the weaves that uses a secondary thread. Figure 3.4 shows an overshot draft.

So, you love this design and decide that you're going to weave a table runner. The warp is 10/2 perle cotton and the pattern weft is 5/2 perle cotton. Immediately you should note that your pattern weft is twice the size of the warp. That will be the first factor that will elongate your image. If you use a fuzzy, soft pattern thread, it will beat in tighter than cotton, but it is still thicker. But then you have to add in a tabby thread—another thread added into the weft that will elongate the image even more. Normally the tabby is the same as the warp, so in this example you would be using 10/2 perle cotton. You can minimize this distortion somewhat by using 20/2 cotton instead of 10/2. That will help—to a point. Many computer programs allow you to add the tabby and adjust the size of the threads, but there

is only so much a computer program can do. Nothing works quite as well as experience and sampling.

What can you do if you want this image to appear as it is on the computer? The easiest solution is to eliminate some repeats. Look at the treadling and you can see that treadles 2, 3, and 4 are all repeated three times. Try repeating them two times instead and see whether you are closer to the look you want. Or change your pattern thread to something softer that will beat in tighter.

This will be an issue with several different methods of weaving, such as summer and winter, crackle, or even lace patterns. As a weaver, you must decide what is most important.

There is one other issue that might be a problem when using the computer to design. You've picked your pattern and love the design. You have also chosen your fiber and are ready to go. Just take one more precaution. Put the design into the computer program and match the colors as best you can. Then zoom out of the image until the threads in the picture are approximately the size of the threads you will be using. This will give you a better picture of the finished product. It can happen that the design that you loved is lost once you start weaving. The fix may be as simple as a color change, one with a higher contrast. Or you may have to use a thicker thread. There are no guarantees with this technique, but it can be a useful tool for your decision making.

Remember that a computer program is there to *aid you and help you to design*. It should not and cannot take the place of experience, sampling, and common sense. Any time I see a computer-generated pattern that has not included an actual woven piece, I pause. I study that pattern, and if it is something I really want to weave, I will sample—and this is coming from someone who really dislikes sampling!

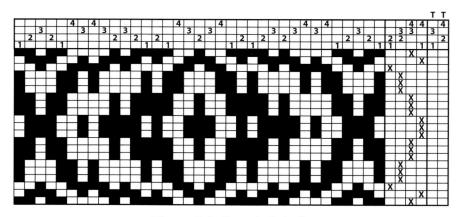

Figure 3.4. Overshot draft.

CHAPTER 4

Fiber Choices

There are many fiber options for the weaver to choose from for weaving towels. Here I'll discuss some of the advantages and drawbacks of each.

Cotton, Unmercerized and Mercerized

For a towel, unmercerized cotton is my fiber of choice. Mercerization is a process the makes the fiber smoother and able to take dye more easily, but this process also makes the fiber less absorbent. Unmercerized cotton has a matte finish, can be a bit fuzzier, and is duller in color. But it does have a great hand and comes in a huge variety of colors and sizes. 8/2 unmercerized cotton is the most common for a towel. 8/4 cotton, also called rug warp, is another good choice. It is a bit heavier but makes a great towel. You could be ambitious and make one-of-a-kind bath towels using 8/4 cotton. 6/2 cotton is also available and would make a wonderful towel.

Mercerized cotton is also known as perle cotton. Because the perle cotton takes the dye better, the colors will be more vibrant. Just think about the color difference between cotton from Lunatic Fringe and unmercerized cotton.

Then the question arises: Can I use perle cotton for a towel? The answer is yes! I often use perle cotton for towels if I want the bright colors or it fits my design better. These towels may not be as absorbent at first, but the more they are washed, the more absorbent they will become.

Mixing perle cotton and unmercerized cotton can also be done. If you create stripes in the warp alternating perle and unmercerized cotton, you may get a seersucker effect when washed, but that could be quite nice. Make it a design element. If you alternate perle

and unmercerized *threads* in the warp, you should have no problem because the fibers are so close. If you use perle cotton for warp and unmercerized cotton for weft, or vice versa, you shouldn't have any problems because the shrinkage will be in different directions.

Organic Cotton

I was very excited to find organic cotton to weave with. American Maid organic cotton is a GMO-free cotton. There is no use of pesticides or chemicals, and it is grown in natural colors. You will find colors in Natural, Light Brown, Dark Brown, Light Green, and Dark Green. There is also bleached organic cotton, which is White. When you first look at some of the organic cotton, you may think there is very little color. Once you have finished your project, soak it in water to which you have added some baking soda. The alkaline solution gives the color a boost. Plus, colors will become more pronounced as you wash your item. Organic cotton is available in different sizes and has a wonderful hand. You can use organic cotton for many projects.

Another organic cotton is Pakucho cotton. This variety is grown in Peru, where GMOs are banned. Pakucho is a Fair Trade product, which means that the people involved in its manufacture are paid a fair living wage and have good working conditions. Pakucho is also a naturally pigmented fiber and is available in Desert Mist, Vicuna, Sage, Forest Mist, and Chocolate. The colors are more intense than the American Maid organic cotton.

Both of these brands of cotton are wonderful to use for towels. They are exceptionally soft and absorbent. You could also use them for baby blankets or wonderful spring shawls.

Cottolin

Cottolin is a blend of cotton and linen. The addition of the linen makes it a very strong and absorbent fiber. The colors are very vibrant, which also makes it desirable. It is a wonderful choice for towels. In my experience, I have found that the shrinkage was more than I expected, so when I use cottolin, I adjust the patterns to allow for this excess shrinkage.

Take the same precautions mixing cotton and cottolin as you would when mixing perle cotton and unmercerized cotton. Shrinkage may be different for each fiber, and you may not be pleased with your results.

Linen

Linen is a very strong fiber and takes color easily, so it can be very vibrant. Linen is very absorbent and dries quickly and thus makes wonderful towels. It is also long wearing, which is why we often see linen towels and table runners at antique shops. But it has the reputation of being difficult to work with. I have not found it to be a problem.

Linen has very little elasticity, so you won't have the stretch you would have with cotton. But it also has very little shrinkage. It can abrade when weaving, so it is good to advance your warp often. I was taught to mist the warp as I wove. If you do this, be sure to let it dry before winding your finished fabric onto itself. When winding a bobbin, I use a damp cloth for the linen to slide through so that the weft thread is also damp. But it is important that you empty that bobbin, as linen will mold. Remember—damp, not wet!

Take the same precautions when mixing fibers, as the shrinkage will be different. Use one fiber for warp and the other for weft. Don't be afraid to weave with linen!

Figure 4.1. Cotton Clouds has a gorgeous array of cotton threads in various weights.

PHOTO BY JESSICA YBARRA, COTTON CLOUDS, INC.

Color, Texture, and Pattern

When designing towels or any other project, there are three design elements you need to keep in mind: color, texture, and pattern. You can combine two of these details, but when/if you add the third, your piece might be "overdesigned." One or more of the details can get lost.

Color

Hand towels are perfect projects for experimenting with color. You can try different color combinations that you wouldn't otherwise use or just try something new. You might even find a new favorite color combination. Because the towels are small, you haven't invested a lot of time into them.

The color wheel has three primary colors: red, blue, and yellow. Secondary colors are mixtures of the primary colors. Mix red and blue, and you will get purple. Mix red and yellow, and you will get orange. Mix blue and yellow, and you will get green. Further mixing of the secondary colors will create the tertiary colors.

The reds, oranges, and yellows are called the warm colors. They remind us of sunshine and heat. These colors will brighten your room and quickly become a focal point. The greens, blues, and purples are called the cool colors. They remind us of the ocean and cool water. These colors are peaceful and calm. Keep all of this in mind when you are choosing colors for your project. If it is a towel, where will they be used? Do you want a pop of color in that room? Or would you prefer a cooler, more serene feeling?

It is important to remember that mixing opposites, or complementary colors, on the color wheel can be a problem. Blending these colors will often result in a muddy look. That doesn't mean that it can't be done—you just have to be careful. Think of Christmas red and Christmas green. One way to keep the colors from becoming muddy is to separate them with white. Keep the areas where the red and green blend together to a minimum. The use of the neutral, white, really makes the red and green pop. This idea will work for any of the complementary colors.

Remember, the smaller the threads are, the more the eye will blend the colors together. Complementary colors are used a lot by sports teams, so if that isn't the look you are going for, you may want to change colors or add a third color.

Analogous colors are very popular in weaving. These colors are side by side on the wheel. Any towel that

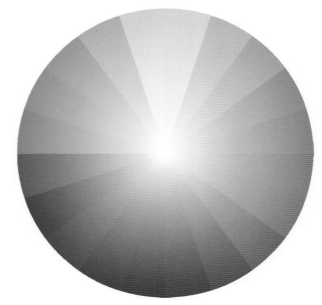

Figure 5.1. Color wheel.

uses blues, greens, and purples is a hit! Try using blue and green, and then pick a third color that moves into the yellows for a pop of color. Working with analogous colors is always successful. This is a great place to start if you want to try something different.

Triadic colors are evenly spaced around the color wheel. They often are very bright and forceful. Combinations can include red, blue, and yellow or green, purple, and orange. Using a neutral like natural or white will keep these combinations from being overpowering.

Any color on the color wheel can be used as a tint, shade, or tone. A tint is a pure color that has white added. A shade is a pure color that has black added. A tone is a pure color that has gray added.

If using color really scares you, study paintings by the old masters. Pick your favorite artist and pull your color palette from his pictures. After you have done this a few times, you will begin to have more confidence in your own color choices.

Color gamps are wonderful learning tools. I have many of them in different colors, fibers, and weave patterns. You can make a color gamp by choosing your favorite colors or colors that you use the most. Create warp stripes that are at least 1.5 inches (3.8 cm) wide in each color. When you weave your gamp, you will weave with those same colors and in squares that are approximately the same size as the width.

So why would I bother to do this? Let's assume you have chosen 12 colors for your warp. You begin weaving with one of those colors, creating a square. Now you will have one square that is a pure color. But the rest of the squares will be a blend of that color and the other 11 colors. This pattern will continue as you work your way through each of the colors. Then, when you are planning another project and deciding on colors, you can refer to your gamp and see how your color choices interact. Did you like the mix on the gamp? Great, you can use it! But if you didn't, you can make the changes now.

Figure 5.2. Place color selections side by side to visualize how they might work together, but then be sure to sample to see how the threads look when woven together in your chosen pattern.

Figure 5.4. Close-up of Spring and Fall towels (page 95).

Figure 5.3. Color Gamp towels, page 179.

Color gamps are woven in plain weave and twill. Why two different weaves? Plain weave is an over and under of one thread. Twill is over and under at least two threads, which means the colors will interact in a different way. I have given you a set of towels that are color gamps (Figure 5.3). You can use them as towels, or you can tuck them away for reference. One towel is woven in plain weave and the other as a 2/2 twill. These towels are a good exercise in color.

Texture

Texture is the feel or look of the surface of a fiber or fabric. Consider the fibers we weave with. Which ones have texture? Boucle, eyelash, mohair, and wool are just a few of the fibers available. Always keep in mind the end use of your project. Since this book is on towels, you would not use a blend of mohair and wool, as that combination would shrink and not be absorbent. That mixture would be more appropriate when weaving a scarf or shawl. Using dark wool with a light-colored bamboo could be striking. The scarf would be using two of the design elements: color and texture!

If you want to add texture to a towel, look for a cotton boucle! Something as simple as mixing a heavier thread (8/4 cotton) with a lighter thread (8/2 cotton) will give you texture in your towel. Look at the Spring and Fall sets of towels (Figure 5.4). In each of these there are additional passes of the 8/2 cotton in the same shed, creating the appearance of a larger thread. These towels have texture!

Pattern

Pattern is the last element in design and is probably the one we have the most fun with since there are so many different weaves that we have to choose from. M's and W's, huck lace, twills—these are all patterns we use in weaving. Using color with these patterns heightens the designs, making them more prominent. Towels are perfect for practicing a new weave pattern and playing with color at the same time.

When you are designing your own towels, keep all of this in mind. But these are your towels, and you should feel free to break a few rules. Some of my more successful projects came about from rule-breaking and accidental mistakes. Have fun with whatever you design.

6

Hemming

Fringe for towels is not recommended, although if you do want a fringe, make it a short fringe, as over time it will wear away. The best way to finish towels is with a rolled hem. I allow a minimum of 1.5 inches (3.8 cm) of plain weave before I start my pattern. If the pattern is twill, I will do 1.5 inches (3.8 cm) of twill pattern. There may be times when a separate plain weave or twill is unnecessary. For example, when weaving Stripes and Diamonds (page 121), instead of weaving for a separate hem, I just wove the entire length of the towel in the pattern and then created a rolled hem.

Now back to the 1.5 inches (3.8 cm) I allow for hemming. This gives me 0.5 inch (1.3 cm) to do the first turn, 0.5 inch (1.3 cm) for the second turn. The second turn conceals the first turn and the raw edges. The last 0.5 inch (1.3 cm) becomes a part of the front of the towel.

Now for neatness! While they may just be towels, they should be finished properly, especially if they are to be gifts. One option is to use a product such as HeatnBond Hem. This is an iron-on strip that secures your hem. This is a permanent bond and you do not sew over it.

You can sew your hems on a machine. This is very secure, but the fabric can slip forward while sewing. A walking foot will help considerably, but you still need to be careful. Reducing the tension on the presser foot can help. Just make sure that your stripes, plaids, patterns, and edges line up as you hem. You do not want excess fabric at the end of the stitched line.

My preference for hems is hand sewing. I turn my hems and hand sew them, using sewing thread. You can use the same fiber that you wove with, but I have found that these threads show more. Sewing thread is very easy to conceal. Hand sewing allows me to make sure that my designs and stripes line up perfectly. I find sewing hems to be a great project for the evening!

CHAPTER 7
Tips, Terms, and Troubleshooting

This section is full of different tips to help you through problems you might have. Some of these solutions are mine, but I do not take credit for all of them. That is one of the wonderful things about going to classes: you learn from others! I've also included definitions of some terms that weavers struggle with. I hope you find these helpful.

Your weaving library

I was recently asked what I felt were the books every weaver should have in their collection. These are my recommendations and reasoning:

Learning to Weave by Deborah Chandler—always good for basic information.

A Handweaver's Pattern Directory by Anne Dixon— wonderful source of 4-shaft patterns.

A Handweaver's Pattern Book by Marguerite Davison—a great book of 4-shaft patterns. Just remember that she used a countermarch loom. This book can be hard to get but is worth it.

A Weaver's Book of 8-Shaft Patterns by Carol Strickler—a great source for weavers with 8-shaft looms.

A Weaver's Companion by Marilyn Murphy—a wonderful tool to keep handy. Murphy has compiled basic information and made it easy to find quickly. Keep this one at the loom!

The project calls for 8/4 or 5/2 cotton, but I don't have that, and I need only a small amount, too!

Substitution is a part of a weaver's life. Let's assume that the pattern calls for 8/4 cotton in red and you don't have that. It calls for only 25 yards (22.9 m) of 8/4 cotton, and you don't want to purchase a whole mini cone just to get those 25 yards (22.9 m). I totally understand that. The easiest solution is to use two strands of a smaller cotton.

If you un-ply 8/4 cotton, you will see that it is made up of 4 strands. If you un-ply 8/2 cotton, you will see that it is made up of 2 strands. So this substitution is easy. But how to do it becomes the question. There are three ways:

1. You could use a shuttle that holds two bobbins. Put 8/2 cotton on each bobbin and weave with this.
2. You could wind two strands of the 8/2 cotton onto one bobbin. This method does have its problems, however. It is very difficult to wind it exactly right, so one thread always seems to be longer than the other. This can be fussy!
3. This solution incorporates a floating selvedge. Wind one bobbin with 8/2 cotton. Once you have passed the shuttle through the shed the first time, beat, wrap the fiber around the floating selvedge, and then back through the same shed. Voilà! You have two threads in that shed, which gives you the correct size you need.

Substituting and changing fibers

Substitution decisions depend on how and where. Standard sizes for the most used perle/mercerized cotton are 20/2, 10/2, 5/2, and 3/2. Unmercerized cotton is 8/2, 6/2, 8/4, and 8/16. The first thing to remember is that changing thread size will change the sett for your project. It will also change the amount of fiber that is needed, so you will need to recalculate for the entire project. Make sure that your substitution is appropriate to the project. You wouldn't use wool for a towel.

1. What is the sett now, and what is the sett for the fiber you want to use?
2. How does this change the width of the project? Do you need to increase or decrease the number of repeats or possibly add a border?
3. If you are not changing the length of the project, then the warp length will not be affected.
4. Count the number of ends for the new fiber and multiply that times the length of the warp to get the yardage needed.
5. For the weft, I go by what should be the ppi for that particular fiber. If the width in the loom is 15 inches (38.1 cm), I calculate for 16 inches (40.6 cm). It's always better to have extra. If my ppi is 20, I multiply that times 16 to get the length needed for 1 inch (2.5 cm). Then multiply that times the number of inches in the project. This gives you the total in inches, so you will need to divide that figure by 36 to get yards.

Changing the fiber is not difficult! Just take your time and work through the process.

Warping board or warping mill?

This is a personal preference. I prefer a warping mill. I do a lot of weaving, and a warping mill is easier on my shoulders. Mills cost more, but this is the one weaving tool that I find is worth every penny. They come in different sizes and are collapsible, so they take no more space than a warping board.

Multiple colors in the warp

So, you have this pattern that you love and it has a lot of color changes in the warp. Patterns will tell you only the number of ends needed per color. This is necessary so that yardage needed can be calculated. There are two ways to approach a colorful warp. The first is to wind each color separately and then dress the loom. This can be faster at first but might be more troublesome later.

I dress the loom from front to back, which means the reed is sleyed first. When I'm winding a colorful warp, I study the pattern to see the arrangement of the threads. Let's look at Figure 7.1.

When I wind my warp, I would begin by winding four white plus one for a floating selvedge. Then I would break the thread, tie on purple and wind eight purple, break the thread and wind eight white, continuing until I have wound the correct number of threads plus the last floating selvedge. Know that you can break the thread and tie on the new one at either end. Now when I go to the loom to sley the reed, the threads are already in the correct order. Plus, I can count my threads to make sure that I have the right number of each color. This may be slower, but I find in the end it is more accurate. You will have to decide what works best for you.

Multiple color changes in the weft

Changing colors when weaving can cause a buildup along the edge, which distorts the fabric. And multiple color changes can slow down the weaving process. When I have a project with multiple color changes, this is how I handle it: I cut my fiber, leaving at least a 3-inch (7.6-cm) thread hanging loose. Then I change the color, again leaving a 3-inch (7.6-cm) piece, and continue to weave. When the project is done, I use a large-eye needle and carefully weave these long threads into the fabric approximately 0.5 inch (1.3 cm). I trim these threads a bit but do the final trimming after the washing to allow for shrinkage. This is a great evening TV project, and it goes faster than you might think.

Let's assume that the color changes are short and just alternating two colors, as in a check. If the color change is less than 0.5 inch (1.3 cm), I will carry the unused

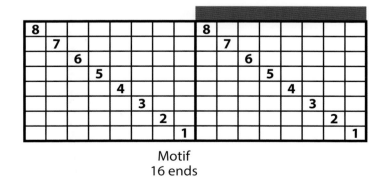

Motif
16 ends

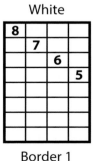

White

Border 1
4 ends

Figure 7.1

color along the edge. You will have a small loop when you do this, but once it is washed, you won't see it at all. Another option is to wrap the thread you are carrying around the thread you are using. This prevents the small loop and holds the thread closer to your piece.

Adding a new bobbin

This follows along with the previous section, except here I am referring to just running out of a thread on a bobbin and needing to splice in a new thread. Unless I am in a Sheep to Shawl competition, I *never* splice in a new thread in the center of the project. All splices will be within 1 inch (2.5 cm) or less of the edge. And I try to keep them as small and neat as possible. We all know our eyes go to those splices, so let's keep them as far from the center as we can. Try to separate the plies in the fiber. Then overlap so that the join has the same number of plies as the original thread.

Working with a new draft

You've chosen a new draft and are anxious to start. I'm the same! But the first thing I do is put that draft into my computer program. One reason is that I want to check the draft for errors. Mistakes happen! As much as we try to avoid them, they still pop up. Nothing is more frustrating than to have the loom threaded and start weaving only to find a problem. Word of caution here: Never upload a draft from a book into a public domain site. There are copyright laws, and you can get into trouble. Just use your personal weaving program.

Putting the draft into a computer program allows you to see the back of the project and check for floats. Maybe you are contemplating a color change? The computer program will allow you to try different combinations and find the perfect one. You can also play with the threading and treadling and possibly find something that you like better. Utilize those computer programs.

Keep a hand mirror handy

While this advice may sound strange, there is a reason. How many times have we gotten our projects off the loom only to discover an error that shows on the wrong side? That is so frustrating! If you keep a hand mirror handy, you can check the underside as you go along. Then you will see those long floats or other errors sooner and be able to correct them.

If you don't have a mirror, you can use your phone to take a picture and examine the picture. With this option, you can zoom to get close images. Also, your camera will have a flash, which will help if your lighting is challenging.

Take a picture of the beginning of your weaving

Now why would you do that? Did you ever get to the end of a runner or scarf and forget how you began? If you take a picture, you can quickly refer to it instead of having to unroll your weaving.

Matching motifs

We've all seen those beautiful ruanas or coverlets and wanted to make one. But then fear sets in. We have to match the motifs! Our beat changes from day to day. Having a bad day, the beat is firmer. Things are going well, the beat is gentler.

So how do we make sure the motifs match? This is where sampling is a good idea. Set up your loom with about 18 inches (45.7 cm) of extra warp. Weave your motif! Is it square? Do you need to make any adjustments? Now is the time to make those decisions. Once you have woven the motif to your satisfaction, you are ready for the next step. Use a small ruler and measure each component of the motif. Let's look at Figure 7.2.

In this motif, I see four areas where I would want to know the dimensions. These are indicated in Figure 7.3.

The first and last sections should be the same length, and the two center sections should be the same length. I make a chart with this information and tape it to my castle. Now I'm ready to weave. Every time I finish one section of the motif, I measure it and check it against my chart. If it is the same, great! If not, then I back it out and weave it again. You will very quickly learn to adjust your beat so that you are not unweaving very often. If you have borders at the beginning and end, make sure you measure those so they are the same! And when you finish, both of your pieces will be the same and match up perfectly.

Sticky shafts

Weather changes affect our looms, some more than others. This past year my shafts just weren't dropping like they should. What to do? 100% silicone spray! I went to the hardware store and found the product shown in Figure 7.4. Note that it is pure silicone with no extra ingredients. You don't want anything that will leave a residue on your loom. I very carefully sprayed this product down along the edges of the shafts. There

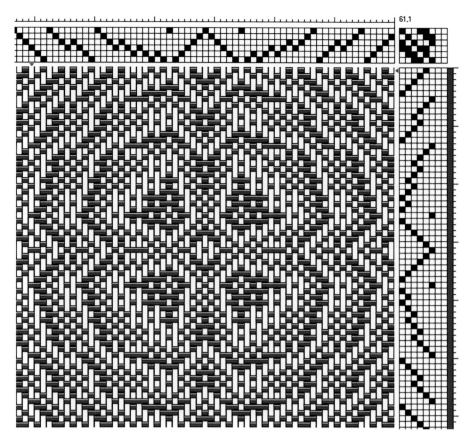

Figure 7.2.

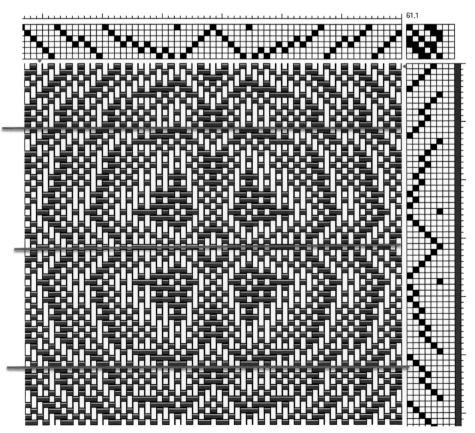

Figure 7.3.

Figure 7.4. Silicone spray is helpful for getting sticky shafts to glide again.

were no problems after that. I'm sure you can find either this spray or something equivalent in your area.

Running out of heddles

This trick works for 8-shaft looms. You are threading your 8-shaft loom with a 4-shaft pattern and realize that you will not have enough heddles on shaft 2. You don't want to move heddles, so what can you do? Use an unused shaft in place of shaft 2. For example, the threads you would have put on shaft 2, now you will put on shaft 8. That's the first part of the problem solved.

Now to the tie-up! We will assume that we are using a basic 2/2 twill tie-up as in Figure 7.5.

		4	4
	3	3	
2	2		
1			1

Figure 7.5. Twill tie-up.

Remember, all of the threads should have been on shaft 2 but now are on both shaft 2 and shaft 8, so when you tie up your loom, any treadle that includes shaft 2 will have to include shaft 8. Figure 7.6 shows your new tie-up. This is much easier than moving heddles!

8	8		
		4	4
	3	3	
2	2		
1			1

Figure 7.6. Twill tie-up using both shaft 2 and shaft 8 for all threads that should have been on shaft 2.

Too many heddles

Again, this solution is for an 8-shaft loom. You are setting it up with a 4-shaft pattern and using the full width. But the heddles on shafts 5 to 8 get in the way. As you thread your heddles on shafts 1 to 4, finish a section and then pull over a few heddles from shafts 5 to 8 and let them ride along. You are spacing those excess heddles as you thread. This approach allows your warp to feed straight and smooth without having problems at the sides.

Keeping track as you weave

This can be a big problem for many weavers. The telephone rings or the bathroom calls. Children interrupt! I've seen many different solutions to this problem, and some are very elaborate. The method I use is very simple and straightforward.

The first thing I do is isolate my treadling repeat. Figure 7.7 shows the treadling for All about Cats (page 175).

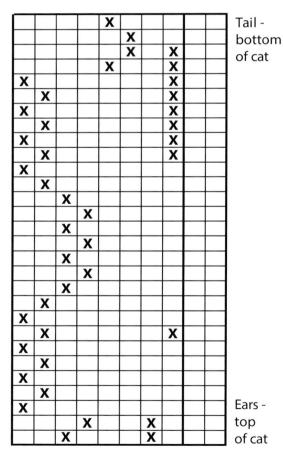

Figure 7.7. Treadling for All about Cats.

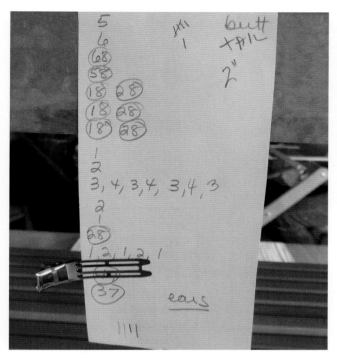

Figure 7.8. My cheat sheet for treadling All about Cats.

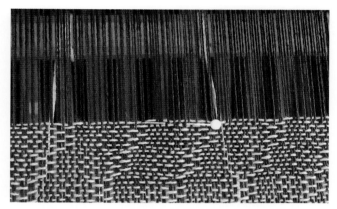

Figure 7.9. Use a straight pin to "underline" the first thread in a repeat.

Having this in front of me is too complicated, so I write it on a piece of paper with my shorthand. Instead of X's, I want to know the treadle numbers. Figure 7.8 shows my "cheat sheet."

The circled numbers indicate when I have to multipedal. But the one thing I really want you to notice is the hair clip! When I start treadling my motif, I put the hair clip under the treadle I need to depress. As I move down my sheet, it is very easy to move the hair clip. If I'm called away from the loom, I make sure the hair clip indicates where I need to start. I keep a pencil handy to make notes. How many inches of plain weave did I start with? I need to end the same way. So you can see my 2 inches (5.1 cm) indicated. This chart also tells me which part of the cat I'm starting with. Other tick marks indicate how many cats I've done, so the second towel is the same. And, yes, this piece of paper goes into my file so when I do another piece with cats on it, I don't have to reinvent my cheat sheet.

Keeping track on the woven piece

This is another area where problems arise, even for the most experienced weaver. We are in the weaving mode, but our thoughts wander and, oh my, where are we? Even with our hair clip we are lost! Or maybe we have discovered an error and now we need to find

it. A simple straight pin with a colorful head is the easy solution.

When I am weaving a motif/pattern, once I have thrown and beat the first thread in the repeat, I "underline" that thread with a straight pin. I like one with a large head and, if possible, a contrasting color.

This straight pin is similar to a lifeline in knitting. I've gotten partway through the motif and am totally lost. Or I've finished the motif and there is an error. The straight pin shows me the beginning of that motif and also tells me that everything before the pin is okay. Now I know that I only have to study the threads after that pin to find the error or where I am in the motif. Pretty simple, right?

Saving and storing fiber

Weavers can spend a lot of money on bobbins. But this isn't necessary. The first solution is to try to not fill your bobbins with any more thread than needed. But that isn't always possible. So here are a couple of alternatives:

- Milkshake straws
- Empty tubes

Figure 7.10. Milkshake straws and empty cardboard tubes can be used as bobbins for extra thread.

Figure 7.11. Hairbands are perfect for securing your extra thread with its cone.

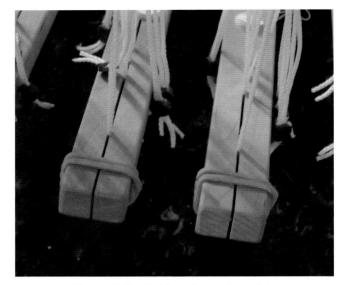

Figure 7.12. Hairbands work well to secure shafts on treadles.

Milkshake straws are larger than regular straws, which is why I recommend those. And they will just fit onto your bobbin winder. You can get two "bobbins" from one straw. Just pop them into the shuttle when needed.

The other option is empty tubes. Don't throw away those hard cardboard tubes when you empty one. They are great for storing that extra thread. You will have to wind it on by hand, but that is easy and fast. And these tubes will fit into some larger shuttles.

So now that you have your thread on one of these "bobbins," how do you keep the thread with the cone? Hairbands—easy to find, inexpensive, very stretchy, and very durable! They are strong enough that the bobbins are held securely and will be with your cone when needed.

Keeping your shafts from coming off the treadles while weaving

This is a problem with some looms. You are happily weaving and then realize the pattern has changed. And then you discover that shaft 8 has come loose from its treadle. Once again, the hairband comes to the rescue! Simply wrap one around the end of the treadle until secure. That shaft won't come off accidentally now. And you can easily remove the hairband when you are finished.

Keeping heddles secured

We have the loom set up, but we haven't used all of the heddles. There are extras on both sides. As we weave, those heddles rub against the outer threads and can abrade those threads. We need to secure them, but it needs to be simple. Binder clips! These clips are easy to put on the shaft. Just make sure the ends point down. They will not interfere with raising and lowering the shafts. Be sure you get the small/mini clips.

Figure 7.13. Mini binder clips hold heddles securely.

Weighting a broken thread or adding floating selvedges

The only time I don't use a floating selvedge is if I am doing plain weave or the piece has plain weave along the sides. Other than that, you will always find a floating selvedge being used. I add those extra threads into my calculation. They are always put into a separate dent, never with another thread and never through a heddle. When I wind on my warp, the floating selvedge is included with the rest of the threads.

If you need to add a floating selvedge later, they are easy enough to add. Let's assume that you have a 3-yard (2.7-m) warp. Cut your floating selvedge 3 yards plus. I would make it 3.5 to 4 yards (3.2 to 3.7 m). I use two empty cones as my weight (Figure 7.14). Wrap the fiber around the first cone, leaving enough to thread through the dent to the front. Then put the second cone over the first. This will secure your thread. These cones have a coating that keeps the threads in place, so this makes them easy to use. After you have secured your thread at the front of your loom, you can let these cones hang from the back of the loom (Figure 7.15). You will need to adjust these cones as you weave. If you are working with Tencel, use two threads together as a floating selvedge. Tencel floating selvedges seem to break more easily.

Figure 7.15.

This is also a good way to weight a thread that has been inserted due to breakage. Wrap the cones as above, but this time you will go through a heddle and a dent. Secure your new thread to your project with a T pin right at the break point. Wrap the new thread around the T pin three or four times, and secure the thread to the cones as above. Then continue to weave. Once your project is done, use a large-eye needle and weave in the end of the broken thread and the end of the new thread for a short distance. After washing, you can trim the ends closely.

Lighting

Good lighting is essential when dressing the loom and weaving. Working with dark threads presents another whole problem. I think I've tried every lamp available.

Figure 7.14.

Figure 7.16. Rechargeable LED headlamp.

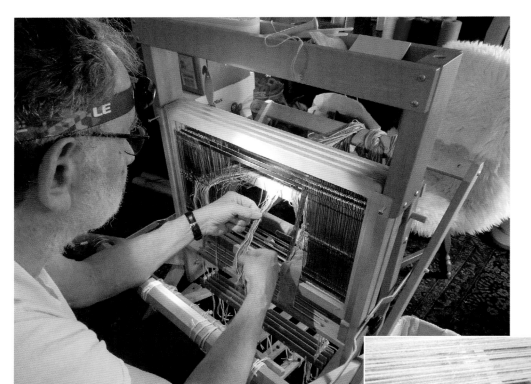

Figure 7.17.
This picture shows you how intense the light is. Since it is attached to your head, the light moves to where you are looking. Just perfect! This was an online purchase.

All of them had good points but were still lacking. Then I discovered the rechargeable LED headlamp. It was just what I was looking for! The strap is very soft and easy to adjust, so it is comfortable. The light has three positions, so you can adjust it to point just where you need it. You will want more than one so that when one needs to be recharged, you have another one ready. They charge quickly by plugging into a USB port. Be sure to get rechargeable lights!

Covering knots

There are many methods used to separate the warp when winding on. My preference is cardboard. At the end of the holidays, a local store puts this brick printed cardboard on sale (Figure 7.18). I'm always there to snap it up. It works perfectly! I have never had a problem with any color transfer. If I need wider cardboard, it is available in rolls from Red Stone Glen.

Now to the front of the loom! Once you have begun weaving, eventually your fabric will wind back onto itself and over the knots at the front. These knots can mess up your tension, so I keep a piece of cardboard that is just long enough to wrap the beam one time. When the fabric gets close to the knots, I insert a piece of cardboard to cover them. This prevents any problems with tension.

Figure 7.18.

Figure 7.19. This piece of cardboard will quickly be out of your way.

Isolating a thread

So, we have discovered that we have a mistake and we have found the thread(s) that need to be corrected. But the surrounding threads get in the way, and it can be ever so frustrating. The simple solution is a comb. The teeth of the comb will hold the threads out of the way while you work with the problem thread. You can put a comb in the back and a comb in the front so that the troublesome thread is isolated in both places.

Figure 7.20. A comb can help isolate an incorrect thread.

Bringing shafts and heddles to eye level

Dressing your loom should not be a back-breaking problem. I dress from front to back so my reed is already sleyed. First, I use a shorter chair or stool at the back of the loom. That lowers me a bit. Then I raise the shafts with either a book or a board (Figure 7.21). This brings the shafts higher and closer to my eye level. And it is much easier on my back. I also remove the back beam so I can get in closer to the heddles.

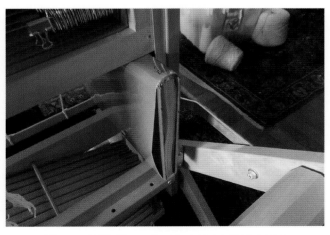

Figure 7.21. Use a book or board to raise the shafts while you dress your loom.

Marking your reeds

A very wise man, Tom Knisely, told me once, "Remember, this is your equipment! Make it work for *you!*" And he is right! I trimmed the legs on my weaving bench so it is just the right height for me. I mark my reeds! Using a silver color Sharpie, I mark the center point and then inch increments to the right and to the left. I also put my name on the reed so if I lend it to someone, they know it is mine. Having these marks eliminates the need to measure every time I'm sleying the reed. I just need to count over the inches and begin. You can also use different colors of duct tape at the ends of your reeds. Use one color for 10 dent reeds and a different color for 12 dent reeds, and so on. This makes them easy to locate when needed.

Figure 7.22. Mark your reeds to make your work easier.

Setting your threads at the beginning of the warp

It is very important when setting your threads to use a thread that is the same size as the warp thread (or one that is very close). I have seen weavers use paper towels or rags. I want you to think about that! Both of these items are considerably larger than the thread you will be weaving with. This does not allow the warp to lay correctly in line when you begin to weave. Look at Figure 7.23. You can see that the threads are spaced widely apart. You will still have to correct this issue before you begin to weave.

I'm going to show you the way I've learned to set the threads. This is the time that I might use that little bit left on a bobbin that isn't useful for anything else. Assuming you have two tabby treadles or something similar, depress one treadle and throw one pass; *do not beat.* Change treadles and throw a second pass of thread, leaving a loop at that side. Then beat both threads at the same time, moving them close to the knots. If you want fringe, allow for that. Figure 7.24 shows the two passes.

Figure 7.23. Rags will not evenly space your threads.

Figure 7.24.

Now look at Figure 7.25, where both threads have been beaten together, firmly, and brought close to the knots or to where you have your fringe allowance.

Figure 7.25.

Notice the difference between Figures 7.23 and 7.25. The threads are more evenly spaced and ready for the next step. At this point you could start weaving your pattern, but I have one more tip for you. Once the threads are set, we often get a "smile" at the edges where the outer threads turn up. How do we eliminate that? Before you cut your waste thread, take it over the front beam and wrap it around the apron rod. Open

your shed and pass the shuttle through and beat into place (Figure 7.26).

Figure 7.26.

Now repeat that wrap on the other side, and then go back through another shed and beat (Figure 7.27).

Figure 7.27.

Now a couple more passes without the wrap, and your warp is set with minimal waste and no smiles (Figure 7.28).

Figure 7.28.

I follow this process every time I set the loom up and have had great success with it.

Figure 7.29. Lightly beat in a piece of ribbon as a spacer to help with hemming.

Preparing for hemstitching

You have your warp set and you have allowed for the fringe, but you still have to hem stitch at the beginning of your piece. Get a length of a slick ribbon. Insert that into a shed and beat lightly into place (Figure 7.29). Now you begin. Weave 0.5 inch (1.3 cm), either tabby or pattern, leaving the long tail to hemstitch with. Gently pull the ribbon out a small amount (Figure 7.30). Be sure to hold onto the warp threads as you do this. You will now have a perfect space to hemstitch in (Figure 7.31). No problem with catching the wrong threads! Keep pulling the ribbon out as you go until you are done. This is a wonderful way to make hemstitching a little bit easier!

Fringes and between projects

In this example, you have your threads set, but you want a fringe. Reclaimed 1-inch (2.5-cm) slats from window blinds are the perfect solution. Insert your first slat, change sheds, and insert your second slat. This would allow for a 2-inch (5.1-cm) fringe. Do you want longer fringe? Add more slats. Begin weaving your project, and then, just as in the prior section, slowly remove the last slat and do your hem stitching. Aren't weavers creative!

Figure 7.30. Pull out the ribbon as you go to reveal a space for hemstitching.

Figure 7.31. This tip makes hemming just a little bit easier.

Keeping selvedges looking good

This is something all weavers strive for, as we should! I am not a production weaver, so being fast is not tremendously important. But I do want the edges to look good. I was taught to "pinch" the thread at the edge after passing the shuttle through the shed (Figure 7.32). I find that my edges turn out fine using this method. And it does not slow me down. If you are having problems with your edges, you might try this approach. Do what works for you!

Figure 7.32. Pinch the thread at the edge after passing the shuttle through the shed to help keep your selvedges even.

Moving heddles

This is a job that I do not enjoy! I always end up with skinned knuckles and a few choice words. But it has to be done. Keeping the heddles in line is the trick. I have found that using a tool designed for holding knitted stitches is perfect. I can slide it next to the shaft bar and through the top or bottom of the heddles. It keeps the heddles in the proper order. If I have to walk away, they will still keep that order. Stitch holders come in all sizes, so you can use the size you need.

Figure 7.33. Knitting stitch holders can hold heddles together in order while you move them.

Some tips on threading

Dressing the loom can be a problem or it can be fun. I enjoy setting up the loom. Over time I have found some tips that make it an easier and more error-free process. Threading the heddles is where most mistakes happen. Since I dress my loom from front to back, I work with my draft upside down.

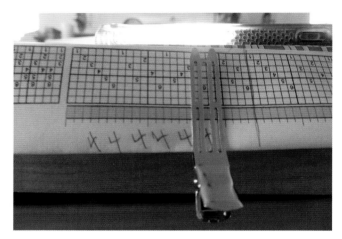

Figure 7.34.

There are some things I want you to see in Figure 7.34. The first thing is that I have isolated my threading repeat. This repeat is short, with only 24 ends. If the repeat is long (as it might be in an overshot threading), I will break it down into workable sections. Next, notice that I have written the number of heddles needed for each shaft. This is important! Also, notice that the hair clip shows up again. I use the hair clip to keep my place. There are also times when I will use two hair clips and bracket the section I'm working on. Now I am ready to start threading the heddles (Figure 7.35).

Figure 7.35.

If you look at Figure 7.34, there were four heddles used on each shaft for this threading. So I am only going to pull over that number of heddles. I lay my warp threads between those heddles and the others so the heddles don't get mixed up. Then I start threading. When I finish that repeat, I should have used all the heddles that I pulled over. If not, there is a mistake! It might be threading, or it could be I miscounted heddles. In either case, I need to locate the problem and make a correction. I won't guarantee that you still won't make mistakes, but doing your threading in small increments like this does lessen the chances. Working in this manner also allows you to walk away and return knowing exactly where you are in the threading draft.

Checking for twisted threads

Once I have the loom dressed and the warp tensioned, the next thing I do is to depress each treadle one at a time. While that shaft is up, I pull the beater bar forward and check that it moves freely and also look behind the beater bar to make sure that there are no twisted threads. These are easily missed, and this is one way to catch them early.

Conserving fiber

One thing I really dislike is wasting fiber! Over the years and from taking many classes, I've learned different ways to tie on to the front and back of the loom. I want to share how I do this since I can generally reduce my warp length by 12 to 18 inches (30.5 to 45.7 cm). That is a lot of fiber!

I dress the loom from front to back. I've sleyed my reed and threaded the heddles. The next thing to do is to tie the warp into 1-inch (2.5 cm) bundles, keeping the knot as close to the end as possible without missing any threads.

Using a strong string, I cut 12-inch (30.5-cm) lengths and tie them to create loops (Figure 7.36). Then these loops are secured around the back rod using a lark's head knot (Figure 7.37). This is much simpler than tying directly to the rod and easier to remove in the future if necessary. I have a loop for each knot. I plan in 1-inch (2.5-cm) increments. These loops stay on my loom!

Next, I create a lark's head knot and put the warp knot through this opening and tighten it down (Figures 7.38 and 7.39). Keep the knot close to the end. Figure 7.40 shows all of the warp threads secured to the back rod. Notice how little of your warp threads are wasted

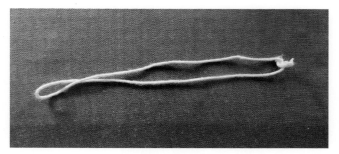

Figure 7.36.

Figure 7.37.

Figure 7.38.

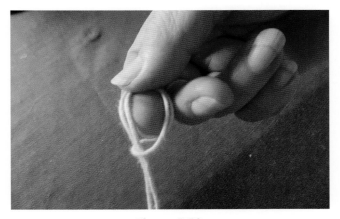

Figure 7.39.

Figure 7.40.

using this method. You are not wrapping around the rod and then tying.

Now I'm ready to beam the warp on. Make sure your knots are all lined up evenly. Always remember to add your cardboard or whatever you use as you beam on. You have wound on the warp and now you move to the front. Trim the ends of the warp so they are all similar in length. I open a shed and finger comb the fibers and make sure everything looks and feels right and the tension is even across the entire piece. Now I tie the warp threads into 1-inch (2.5-cm) bundles. I cut a strong string that is 8 times the width of the project. So, if my piece is 8 inches (20.3 cm) wide, the string is 64 inches (162.6 cm) long. This might sound like a lot, but it gives you ample string to adjust tension. I wrap this string onto a netting shuttle to secure it (Figure 7.41).

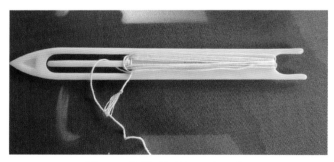

Figure 7.41. Netting shuttle.

Tie one end of that string onto the front rod. Open a shed and put the netting shuttle through the opening in the first 1-inch (2.5-cm) bundle of threads and then around the rod (Figures 7.42 and 7.43). Repeat this across the piece through each thread bundle until you get to the end (Figure 7.44). If you have excess string, don't cut it.

Figure 7.42.

Figure 7.43.

Figure 7.44.

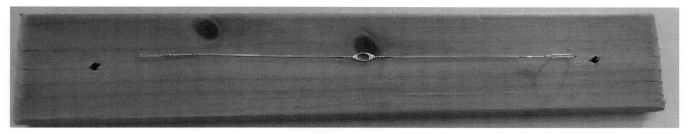

Figure 7.45.

Figure 7.46.

Secure the end of the string and close the shed. Next, work the string with your fingers until it is evenly spaced through the warp bundles. Keep tightening the tension and adjusting the string until the tension is even across the entire piece. This might take some practice, but once you get used to it, it goes quite fast. I save the strings by putting them into bags or small containers and marking them with the length. This way I have them ready to use again. Now you are ready to put in your trash thread. Again, notice how little waste there is with this method instead of wrapping and tying the warp around the front rod.

Emergency heddles

You can purchase emergency heddles, or you can make them yourself with a piece of wood, finishing nails, string, safety pins, and a hammer.

Using one of your heddles, place it on the wood (Figure 7.45) and put nails in the four spots indicated in Figure 7.46. This becomes your jig, or pattern block.

Next, put safety pins on the two outer nails. Thread your string through the hole in the first safety pin and tie securely. Then create the eye hole in the heddle. Make sure to knot on both sides of the nail so the hole doesn't shift. Then thread the string through the last safety pin and secure the thread with a knot.

Remove this from the jig. You now have an emergency heddle that is easy to secure to your shaft with the safety pins (Figures 7.47 and 7.48). Make up a few of these and keep them handy.

Figure 7.47. Emergency heddle.
Figure 7.48. Use the safety pins to secure the emergency heddle to the shaft.

Storage

Now you have made your emergency heddles, guide/length cords for you board/mill, or lashing cords. How can you keep them all organized? The Dollar Store has these wonderful little boxes that come 12 in a package (Figure 7.49). They are perfect for storing all these items. Write the lengths or any other information that you want on the lid, and they will keep your objects safe until you need them again.

Final touches

You have woven your towel and are ready to hem. There is one final touch that will make it extra special: Add tape to one corner so the towel can be hung from a hook. Use ⅜-inch (0.8-cm) fabric tape or grosgrain ribbon cut in 3-inch (7.6-cm) lengths. Look at Figure 7.50 to see how the tape is folded and tucked into the hem. I would still sew the hem by hand but use the machine to further secure the tape. Now you can hang the towel from a drawer handle or hook.

Another finishing touch is to add a personalized label! These can be purchased in many places in all different price ranges. Once again, this is something I would secure by machine. A personalized label is a wonderful reminder of your gift.

Figure 7.49. Small plastic containers are perfect for storing emergency heddles and lashing cords.

Figure 7.50. Adding a piece of tape to the hem allows the towel to hang from a hook or drawer handle.

Figure 7.51. Personalized labels set your work apart.

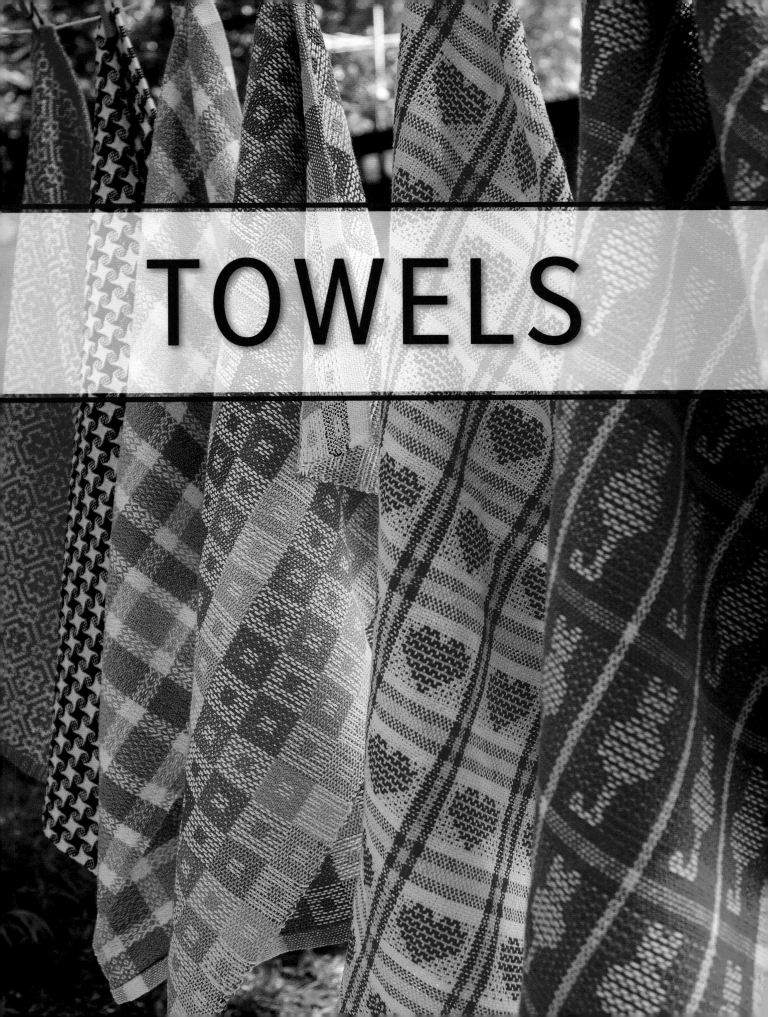

TOWELS

Fiesta Plus One

I grew up in a place where Fiestaware was used every day. We didn't have a lot, and my mother got the plates as rewards from a gas station. A totally different time! But I always loved the bright colors and, as I usually set the table, I made sure I got the color plate I wanted—and gave the color I liked least to my brothers. I still have those plates and have added to our collection with some of the more modern pieces. Those bright colors really add to a kitchen or dining room. So why not have kitchen towels that reflect those colors?

This pattern is easy to set up and easy to weave! I alternated five colors and White, beginning and ending with the White:

- Red–Green–Orange–Blue–Gold

It really makes no difference what sequence you use except that two of the colors will have an extra stripe. You will have a White plain weave on both outer sides. Weave your first towel for 29 inches (73.7 cm). There is no need for a special tabby for hemming. Then put four passes of a high-contrast thread to separate and weave the second towel. Finish each towel with a rolled hem. You will be weaving with the wrong side up and the pattern underneath. This method eliminates raising a lot of heddles. Use a mirror as you weave to see the underside until it rolls around.

The two-color towel shows a totally different effect. You could use any color combination that fits in your home. Also, note that this pattern is a great stash buster. You need only four warp threads of each color per repeat. You could use up a lot of those partial cones in this set of towels. Something to think about!

Enjoy!

Dimensions: 15 inches × 25 inches (38.1 × 63.5 cm)
Sett: 20 epi, 10 dent reed, 2 threads per dent
Length: 3-yard (2.7-m) warp

MULTICOLOR TOWEL

Warp
Threads: 8/2 Cotton Clouds Aurora Earth
- Nassau Blue: 28 ends, 90 yards (82.3 m)
- Kelly Green: 32 ends, 100 yards (91.4 m)
- Gold: 28 ends, 90 yards (82.3 m)
- Dark Red: 32 ends, 100 yards (91.4 m)
- Orange: 28 ends, 90 yards (82.3 m)
- White: 152 ends plus 2 floating selvedges = 154 ends, 475 yards (434.3 m)

Weft
8/2 Cotton Clouds Aurora Earth, White: 525 yards (480 m)

TWO-COLOR TOWEL

Warp
Threads: 8/2 Cotton Clouds Aurora Earth
- Natural: 152 ends plus 2 floating selvedges = 154 ends, 475 yards (411.5 m)
- Rust: 148 ends, 475 yards (411.5 m)

Weft
8/2 Cotton Clouds Aurora Earth, Natural: 550 yards (502.9 m)

Threading
Full Motif: 37 times
Partial Motif: 1 time

White

4			
	3		
		2	
			1

**Partial Motif
4 ends**

Color			White				
8							
	7						
		6					
			5				
				4			
					3		
						2	
							1

**Full Motif
8 ends**

Tie-up and Treadling

			8
		7	
	6		
5			
	4		4
3		3	
	2		2
1		1	
X			
	X		
		X	
			X

Purple Pinwheels

Pinwheel patterns make such a visual statement. These look so complicated but are so very easy. You could make these towels up for Christmas gifts! Make one set red and another set green. Be careful putting red and green in the same towel, as the colors can become muddy looking. These towels would also be the perfect housewarming gift. Weave them up in your friend's favorite colors, and they will be just perfect.

Don't cut your threads each time you change color. Instead, carry the unused color along the side. It won't be a problem for this short distance. Begin each towel with 1 inch (2.5 cm) of plain weave, and then weave 24 inches (61 cm) of the pattern and finish with 1 inch (2.5 cm) of plain weave. Weave three or four passes of a contrasting color to separate the towels and repeat the process for the second towel. Finish each towel with a rolled hem. For this set, I rolled the hem completely to the back of the towel.

The borders for the threading and treadling complete a purple pinwheel, so be sure to use them. If you want wider towels, just add some full motifs to your threading.

Dimensions: 14.5 inches × 24 inches (36.8 × 61 cm)

Warp
Sett: 20 epi, 10 dent reed, 2 threads per dent
Length: 3-yard (2.7 m) warp
Threads: 8/2 Cotton Clouds Aurora Earth
- Purple: 144 ends, 450 yards (411.5 m)
- White: 144 ends plus 2 floating selvedges = 146 ends, 450 yards (411.5 m)

Weft
Threads: 8/2 Cotton Clouds Aurora Earth
- Purple: 275 yards (251.5 m)
- White: 275 yards (251.5 m)

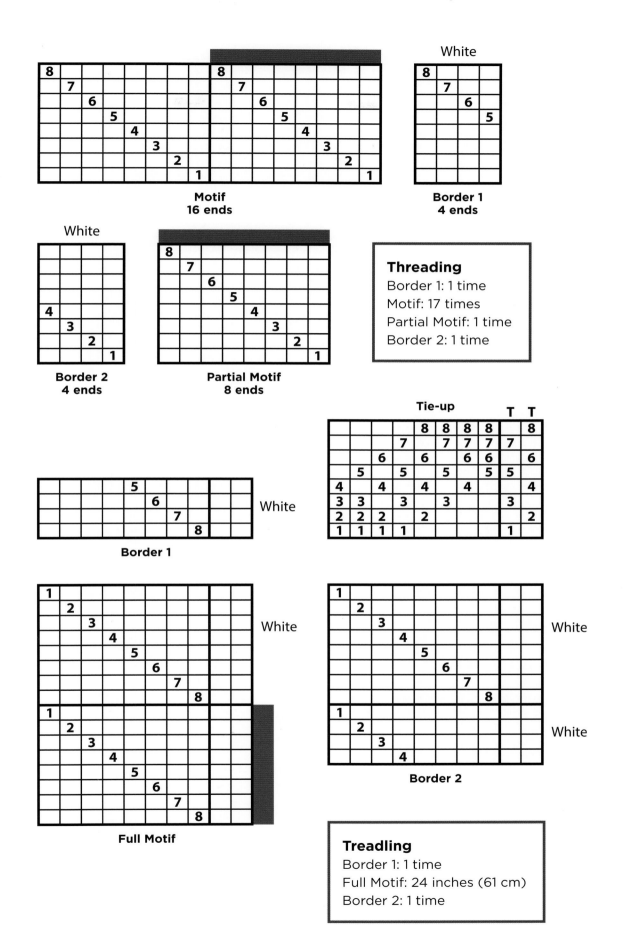

Motif
16 ends

White
Border 1
4 ends

White
Border 2
4 ends

Partial Motif
8 ends

Threading
Border 1: 1 time
Motif: 17 times
Partial Motif: 1 time
Border 2: 1 time

Tie-up

White
Border 1

White
Full Motif

White
White
Border 2

Treadling
Border 1: 1 time
Full Motif: 24 inches (61 cm)
Border 2: 1 time

Sweet and Simple

This set of towels is a very fun and easy set to weave. Both of these towels were woven with the same Dark Navy for the pattern thread. Just use a different color if you want two different-colored towels. This is a summer and winter threading pattern. You will substitute the four-thread pattern for each lettered block.

Block B   Block A

Block Substitution

Using letters instead of writing out the full draft is much easier once you get used to it. But if it is too confusing, just write out the full threading before you begin. When you are weaving, be sure to add a tabby between each pattern thread.

The summer and winter pattern thread is generally twice the size of the warp and tabby. However, for this set I used the same size thread, but just a single strand! You could also use 8/4 cotton for a heavier pattern thread.

Begin your first towel with 1.5 inches (3.8 cm) of plain weave. Then weave the complete treadling pattern one time. Follow with another 1.5 inches (3.8 cm) of plain weave. Weave four passes of plain weave with a high-contrast color to separate the towels. Then repeat the process for the second towel. Finish each towel with rolled hems.

Dimensions: 14.5 inches × 24.5 inches (36.8 × 62.2 cm)

Warp
Sett: 20 epi, 10 dent reed, 2 threads per dent
Length: 3-yard (2.7-cm) warp
Thread: 8/2 Cotton Clouds Aurora Earth, White: 296 ends plus 2 floating selvedges = 298 ends, 900 yards (823 m)

Weft
Pattern thread: 8/2 Cotton Clouds Aurora Earth, Dark Navy: 500 yards (457.2 m)
Tabby: 8/2 Cotton Clouds Aurora Earth, White: 500 yards (457.2 m)

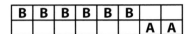

Full Motif
32 ends

Partial Motif
8 ends

Threading
Full Motif: 9 times
Partial Motif: 1 time

Treadling
Weave the full treadling once. Add tabby between each pattern thread.

Tie-up and Treadling

T T

		4	4		4	
3	3				3	Tie-up
		2		2	2	
1		1		1		
X						
	X					Repeat 3X
	X					
X						
		X				
			X			Repeat 6X
			X			
		X				
X						
	X					Repeat 3X
	X					
X						
		X				
			X			Repeat for 20 in (51cm)
			X			
		X				
X						
	X					Repeat 3X
	X					
X						
		X				
			X			Repeat 6X
			X			
		X				
X						
	X					Repeat 3X
	X					
X						

Coffee Time

How fun are these coffee mugs! These would be the perfect towels to use when you serve coffee to friends and family. I chose to use a doubled 8/2 thread for the coffee cups. One towel uses the color Beauty Rose, and the second towel is in Dark Red. Since the motif uses so little yardage, this is a good way to use up those small amounts that we all have. You can also use 8/4 carpet warp, but you will need only half of the yardage indicated for 8/2 thread. Try different color cups at each end of the towel for a whimsical look.

Begin each towel with 2 inches (5 cm) of plain weave in White. Then four passes of Beige, six passes of White, and then begin the motif. Follow the motif with five or six passes of White and then four passes of Beige. After this step, weave 2 inches (5 cm) of White, followed by four passes of Beige. Repeat six times. Then, following the same pattern as in the beginning, weave the second set of coffee cups. Insert four passes of a high-contrast thread and begin the second towel. Finish each towel with a rolled hem.

You must remember: The coffee cup motif is directional! The treadling is marked with the base of the cup. Make sure that the directions of the cups are correct as you are weaving! For the first set of towels, read the chart from the top down. For the second set of towels, read the chart from the bottom up.

The finishing touch on these towels is the steam rising up from each cup. I used Brown 8/4 carpet warp and hand embroidered the steam, making sure each one was different. After all, no cup of coffee is the same.

Dimensions: 14.5 inches × 24 inches (35.6 × 61 cm)

Warp

Sett: 20 epi, 10 dent reed, 2 threads per dent
Length: 3-yard (2.7-m) warp
Threads: 8/2 Cotton Clouds Aurora Earth
- White: 256 ends plus 2 floating selvedges = 258 ends, 850 yards (800.1 m)
- Beige: 36 ends, 125 yards (114.3 m)

Weft

Pattern threads: 8/2 Cotton Clouds Aurora Earth
- Dark Red: 45 yards (41.2 m)
- Beauty Rose: 45 yards (41.2 m)

Beige stripe: 40 yards (36.6 m)
Tabby and plain weave: 8/2 White: 600 yards (548.6 m)
Hand-embroidered steam: 8/4 Brown cotton rug warp: 5 yards (4.6 m)

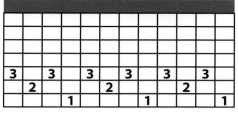

Border 1
12 ends

Threading
Border 1: 1 time
Alternate Motifs A and B: 3 times
Motif A: 1 time
Border 2: 1 time

Repeat 7X

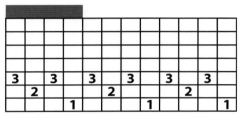

Motif A
56 ends

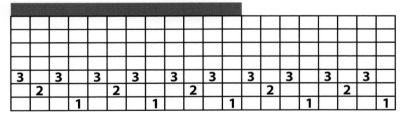

Motif B
12 ends

Tie-up and Treadling

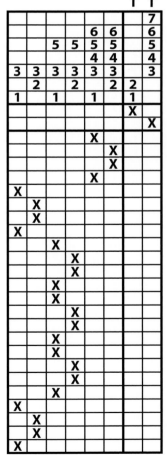

Base of cup

Top of cup

Border 2
12 ends

Treadling
See instructions in
text on page 57.
Add tabby between
each pattern thread.

Simply Twill

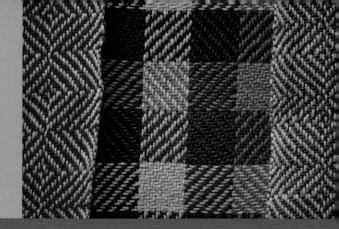

These sets of towels are woven in a broken twill pattern. Looking at it one way, you see squares. But look again and you will see diamonds! Light colors make the pattern soft and muted, where bright, dark colors will make the pattern more prominent.

For the first set, I used a White warp. This choice allows you to change the color just by using a different color weft thread. I chose Blue for one towel and Lipstick for the second. The yardage for the warp is for two towels. Maybe you want to make more! Just add 30 inches (76.2 m) for each additional towel. Since a small amount of fiber is needed for the weft, these towels are a great way to use up those small partial cones.

Now the second set! What a difference adding color makes! This set of towels is very bold and colorful. The sequence of color in the warp from right to left is Orange–Purple–Yellow–Green. Each color has a repeat of 16 threads. This sequence is repeated four times and ends with one more Green and Yellow set. This towel is narrower than the two-color towel. It measures 14.5 inches wide in the loom.

Now for treadling! Motifs A and B will be different colors. Following the same color sequence, weave Motif A in Green, Motif B in Yellow, Motif A in Purple, and Motif B in Orange. Repeat this sequence seven times, and end with one more repeat of Motif A in Green.

Begin your towels with 1.5 inches (3.8 cm) of tabby. For the first set, the tabby is White, and for the second set, the tabby is Yellow. But do note that since this is a broken twill, the tabby will not be a true tabby. There will be sections of doubled warp threads. This result is normal in a broken twill. Now you can weave your first towel. End with another 1.5 inches (3.8 cm) of plain weave followed by four passes of a high-contrast color to separate the towels. Then weave the second towel. Finish your towels with a rolled hem.

Dimensions: 15 inches (14.5 inches for multicolor set) × 23 inches (38.1 × 58.4 cm)
Sett: 20 epi, 10 dent reed, 2 threads per dent
Length: 3-yard (2.7 m) warp

BLUE/LIPSTICK SET

Warp

8/2 Cotton Clouds Aurora Earth, White: 306 ends plus 2 floating selvedges = 308 ends, 950 yards (868.7 m)

Weft

8/2 Cotton Clouds Aurora Earth
- Blue: 300 yards (274.3 m)
- Lipstick: 300 yards (274.3 m)

MULTICOLOR SET

Warp

8/2 Cotton Clouds Aurora Earth
- Green: 80 ends plus 1 floating selvedge = 81 ends, 250 yards (228.6 m)
- Orange: 64 ends, 200 yards (182.9 m)
- Purple: 64 ends, 200 yards (182.9 m)
- Yellow: 80 ends plus 1 floating selvedge = 81 ends, 250 yards (228.6 m)

Weft

8/2 Cotton Clouds Aurora Earth
- Green: 150 yards (137.2 m)
- Orange: 100 yards (91.4 m)
- Purple: 100 yards (91.4 m)
- Yellow (also used for hems): 150 yards (137.2 m)

Border 1
8 ends

4	3	2	1	4	3	2	1
4				4			
	3				3		
		2				2	
			1				1

Full Motif
24 ends

(Threading repeat: 3, 4, 1, 2 — repeated 6 times)

3	4	1	2	3	4	1	2	3	4	1	2	3	4	1	2	3	4	1	2	3	4	1	2

Border 2
10 ends

(Threading repeat: 1, 2, 3, 4)

1	2	3	4	1	2	3	4	1	2

Threading
Border 1: 1 time
Full Motif: 12 times
Border 2: 1 time

Treadling
See instructions in text on page 61 for the set you want to make.

Tie-up and Treadling

Tie-up (top), Motif A and Motif B treadling (X marks) follow below.

Motif A

Motif B

Shuttles

Such a fun set of towels for weavers! If you have a studio or shop, wouldn't these be perfect for the restroom? You could also make a wonderful table runner with this pattern. This would be a perfect gift for a weaving friend. I do have a word of caution if you decide to change the Nile Green color: A darker thread in this section can overpower the shuttle, and you may not be pleased with the result. Learn from my experience! However, each Nile Green or light stripe takes only 30 yards (27.4 m), so this would be a good project to use up those partial cones of light color thread.

Begin your towels with 2 inches (5.1 cm) of plain weave in Natural. Then weave 4 Kelly Green, 6 Nile Green, 4 Kelly Green. Now you are ready to start the Motif Block. Weave four passes of Natural, and then start the shuttle. Be sure to put a tabby after each pattern thread. After completing the shuttle, weave four passes of Natural and another set of stripes. For the center section, weave 2.5 inches of Natural, a set of stripes and 2.5 inches (6.4 cm) of Natural. Beginning with the stripes, repeat the Motif section. Finish with 2 inches (5.1 cm) of plain weave. Weave four passes with a high color contrast to separate the towels, and repeat the whole process for the second towel. Finish your towels with a rolled hem.

Dimensions: 15 inches × 23 inches (38.1 × 58.4 cm)

Warp

Sett: 20 epi, 10 dent reed, 2 threads per dent
Length: 3-yard (2.7-m) warp
Threads: 8/2 Cotton Clouds Aurora Earth
- Natural: 240 ends, 750 yards (685.8 m)
- Kelly Green: 30 ends plus 2 floating selvedges = 32 ends, 125 yards (114.3 m)
- Nile Green: 35 ends, 125 yards (114.3 m)

Weft

Stripes: 8/2 Cotton Clouds Aurora Earth
- Natural: 475 yards (434.3 m)
- Kelly Green: 35 yards (32 m)
- Nile Green: 35 yards (32 m)

Pattern Thread: 8/4 cotton, Dark Brown: 125 yards

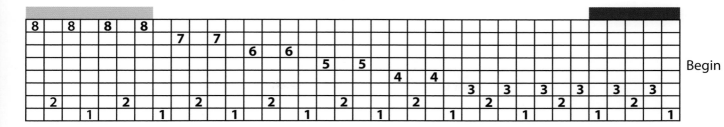

Begin

End

**Full Motif
60 ends**

**Partial Motif
5 ends**

Tie-up and Treadling

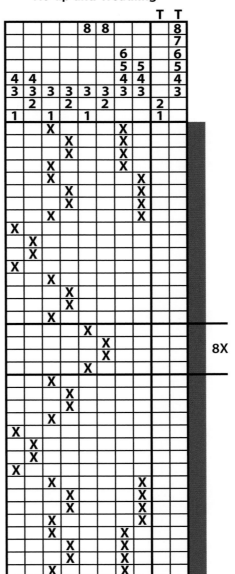

8X

Threading
Repeat Full Motif:
  5 times
Partial Motif: 1 time

Treadling
See instructions in
text on page 63.
Follow each pattern
thread with a tabby
thread.

Pakucho Stripes

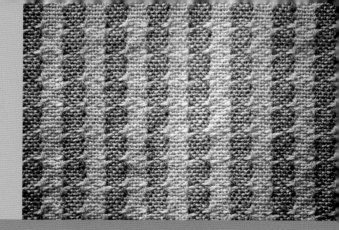

This set of towels is not only beautiful but also very soft! There are four different colors of the Pakucho organic cotton. Each stripe has eight ends. Reading from right to left, the color sequence is as follows: Vicuna–Chocolate–Sage–Forest Mist. This sequence is repeated 11 times, ending with one more Forest Mist stripe.

The weft is Pakucho 10/2 in Desert Mist, which is the lightest of all the colors. This 8-shaft pattern is just perfect for this cotton. It's easy to thread, easy to treadle, but has just enough pattern to be stunning. There are tiny floats that sparkle like little diamonds!

You will notice in the tie-up that some of the tie-ups are duplicated. While that may seem strange, it also allows you to walk the treadles from one to eight without having to search to get the proper treadle.

There is no need for a special treadling for the hem. Just weave until your piece is 28 or 29 inches (71.1 or 73.7 cm), and then weave four passes of a high-contrast color to separate the towels. Now you can weave the second towel. Finish your towels with a rolled hem. You will find that the blocks that are created while weaving give you the perfect place to fold your towel.

Remember, these are natural cottons, so the more they are washed, the darker the colors become. Won't it be fun to see what the colors are after a year or two of use? I did hand wash my towels in water with one tablespoon of baking soda, which acts to increase the color. Then I soaked them in fabric softener to finish.

Dimensions: 15 inches × 24.5 inches (38.1 × 62.2 cm)

Warp

Sett: 24 epi, 12 dent reed, 2 threads per dent

Length: 3-yard (2.7 m) warp

Threads: 10/2 Cotton Clouds Organic Pakucho Cotton
- Forest Mist: 96 ends plus 2 floating selvedges = 98 ends, 300 yards (274.3 m)
- Sage: 88 ends, 275 yards (251.5 m)
- Chocolate: 88 ends, 275 yards (251.5 m)
- Vicuna: 88 ends, 275 yards (251.5 m)

Weft

10/2 Cotton Clouds Organic Pakucho Cotton, Desert Mist: 700 yards (640.1 m)

Threading, Tie-up, and Treadling

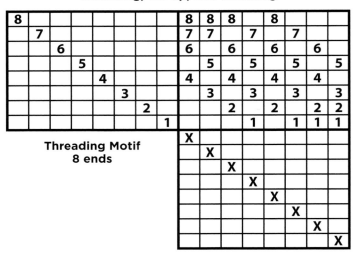

**Threading Motif
8 ends**

Treadling Motif

Stonewashed Squares

This could be the softest set of towels you have ever made! The stonewash cotton has such a soft and absorbent quality. Add to that the variegated color, and it is a win-win for hand towels. This pattern is a simple 8-shaft twill pattern, but if you look closely at the blocks, you can see texture in each one. With the slightly larger weft thread, the stone-washed blocks pop even more.

Although I used a White warp, you might think about one or more colors to give your towels a new and different look. This could be choices from the additional stonewash colors or just a solid 8/2 cotton. Switch things around, play with positions and colors, and see what you can create.

Begin your towel with 1.5 inches (3.8 cm) of plain weave. Next, weave the full motif 19 times, ending with another 1.5 inches (3.8 cm) of plain weave. Weave four passes of a high-contrast thread, and then weave the second towel in the same sequence. Finish each towel with a rolled hem.

Dimensions: 15.5 inches × 24 inches (39.4 × 61 cm)

Warp
Sett: 20 epi, 10 dent reed, 2 threads per dent
Length: 3-yard (2.7-m) warp
Thread: 8/2 Cotton Clouds Aurora Earth, White: 312 ends plus 2 floating selvedges = 314 ends, 950 yards (868.7 m)

Weft
5/2 Cotton Clouds Aurora Earth
• Stonewash Sapphire: 250 yards (228.6 m)
• Stonewash Burgundy: 250 yards (228.6 m)

Threading — Motif: 24 ends

Shaft	1	2	3	4	5	6	7	8	9	10	11	12	13	14	15	16	17	18	19	20	21	22	23	24
8	8		8			8																		
7		7		7			7																	
6			6		6			6																
5				5		5			5															
4										4				4				4						
3											3				3				3					
2												2				2				2				
1													1				1				1			

**Motif
24 ends**

Threading
Motif: 13 times

Tie-up and Treadling

Tie-up (T T mark the tabby treadles)

Shaft	1	2	3	4	5	6	7 (T)	8 (T)
8	8	8	8		8			8
7	7	7		7		7	7	
6	6		6	6		6		6
5		5	5	5			5	5
4	4				4	4	4	
3		3		3	3		3	3
2			2		2	2		2
1				1		1	1	1

Treadling

Row	1	2	3	4	5	6	7	8
1	X							
2		X						
3			X					
4				X				
5	X							
6		X						
7			X					
8				X				
9	X							
10		X						
11			X					
12				X				
13					X			
14						X		
15							X	
16								X
17					X			
18						X		
19							X	
20								X
21					X			
22						X		
23							X	
24								X

Motif

Treadling
Motif: 19 times

Tiny Textured Tiles

A simple threading and a simple treadling, but, oh, what a sweet set of towels. When weaving these towels, don't cut the thread for each color change! Just carry the unused thread along the edge, keeping it close so a loop isn't forming. Once the towels are washed, you will never notice these threads. The little tiles are so small that when you see these towels from a distance, your eye might blend the colors, so instead of seeing blue and yellow, you might see green. A good lesson in color! If you use red and yellow, your eye might see orange.

These towels are woven in pattern for 29 inches (73.7 cm). This is a small pattern, so there is no need to weave a tabby for the hem. After you have woven your first towel, weave four passes of a high-contrast thread for separation. Then weave your second towel. Finish each towel with a rolled hem, making sure that the fold is at the edge of a color.

Dimensions: 15 inches × 25 inches (38.1 × 63.5 cm)

Warp
Sett: 20 epi, 10 dent reed, 2 threads per dent
Length: 3-yard (2.7-m) warp
Threads: 8/2 Cotton Clouds Aurora Earth
- Yellow: 148 ends, 475 yards (411.5 m)
- Light Turk: 152 ends plus 2 floating selvedges = 154 ends, 475 yards (434.3 m)

Weft
8/2 Cotton Clouds Aurora Earth
- Yellow: 300 yards (274.3 m)
- Light Turk: 300 yards (274.3 m)

Full Motif
8 ends

4				4			
	3				3		
		2				2	
			1				1

Threading

Full Motif: 37 times
Partial Motif: 1 time

Partial Motif
4 ends

4			
	3		
		2	
			1

Tie-up and Treadling

4			4
3	3		
	2	2	
		1	1
X			
	X		
		X	
			X
	X		
X			
			X
		X	
X			
	X		
		X	
			X
	X		
X			
			X
		X	

Treadling

Repeat the motif, changing colors after each repeat, for 29 inches (73.7 cm).

Spice Blocks

This set of towels is a summer and winter weave structure. It is written as a profile draft, but don't let that confuse you. Below are the blocks that you will substitute for the letters.

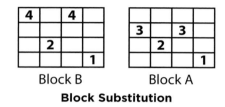

Block B   Block A

Block Substitution

If you look at the Full Motif, you will see 4 Bs at the beginning. You will substitute the threading in Block B 4 times. If you were to write just that part out fully, it would look like the chart below. Feel free to write out the threading completely if that makes you more comfortable.

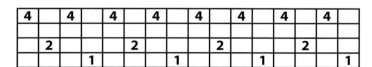

Block B substituted 4 times

I used Natural color cotton for the warp and two different spice colors for the pattern. Instead of using a pattern thread that is larger than the warp, I chose to use the same size thread, and it works just fine. With a neutral warp, you can make these towels any color you want.

Begin your towel with 1.5 inches (3.8 cm) of plain weave. Then repeat the Full Motif five times and end with the Partial Motif once. Next, you will weave another 1.5 inches (3.8 cm) of plain weave. Weave four passes of a high-contrast thread and repeat the process for the second towel. Finish each towel with a rolled hem. Be sure to use a tabby thread after each pattern thread.

Dimensions: 15 inches × 24 inches (38.1 × 61 cm)

Warp

Sett: 20 epi, 10 dent reed, 2 threads per dent
Length: 3-yard (2.7-m) warp
Thread: 8/2 Cotton Clouds Aurora Earth, Natural: 304 ends plus 2 floating selvedges = 306 ends, 925 yards (845.8 m)

Weft

Pattern threads: 8/2 Cotton Clouds Aurora Earth
- Orange: 250 yards (228.6 m)
- Rust: 250 yards (228.6 m)

Tabby: 8/2 Cotton Clouds Aurora Earth, Natural: 550 yards (502.9 m)

Full Motif
72 ends

				B				B				B	B	B	B
A	A	A	A		A	A	A	A		A	A	A	A		

Threading
Full Motif: 4 times
Partial Motif: 1 time

Partial Motif
16 ends

B	B	B	B

Tie-up and Treadling

				T	T
		4	4		4
3	3				3
2		2		2	
	1		1	1	

Full Motif

			X		
		X				3X
		X			
			X		
	X				
X						3X
X					
	X				
			X		
		X				1X
		X			
			X		
	X				
X						3X
X					
	X				
			X		
		X				1X
		X			
			X		
	X				
X						3X
X					
	X				

Treadling
Full Motif: 5 times
Partial Motif: 1 time
Add tabby between each pattern thread.

Partial Motif

			X		
		X				4X
		X			
			X		

Simply Natural

This is a very simple but elegant set of towels. Using the organic cotton for the warp gives them a very soft hand. As these towels are used and washed, the Light Green will be more evident but not overpower the brown used for the overshot pattern. If you want to give the green a boost, just soak your towels in warm water with 1 tablespoon of baking soda before washing. These towels would be a wonderful addition to the guest bathroom!

I used only one repeat of the overshot motif at each end, but you could make this an overall pattern if you preferred. As always, change the colors and make this set your own!

Begin with 2 inches (5.1 cm) of plain weave. Then weave one repeat of the overshot pattern. Follow this step with 15 inches (38.1 cm) of plain weave and one more repeat of the overshot pattern followed by another 2 inches (5.1 cm) of plain weave. Next, weave four passes of a high-contrast color to separate the towels. Repeat the process for the second towel. Finish the towels with a rolled hem. Be sure to put a tabby in between each pattern throw in the motif!

Dimensions: 14 inches × 24.5 inches (35.6 × 62.2 cm)

Warp

Sett: 24 epi, 12 dent reed, 2 threads per dent

Length: 3-yard (2.7-m) warp

Thread: 8/2 Cotton Clouds American Maid Organic Cotton, Light Green: 345 ends plus 2 floating selvedges = 347 ends, 1,100 yards (1,005.8 m)

Weft

Pattern thread: 8/4 cotton, Coffee: 125 yards (114.3 m)

Tabby and plain weave: 8/2 Cotton Clouds American Maid Organic Cotton, Light Green: 650 yards (594.4 m)

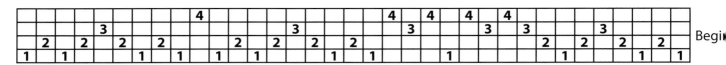

Begin

End

Motif A
51 ends

Motif B
3 ends

Border 1
4 ends

Border 2
4 ends

Tie-up and Treadling

End

Begin

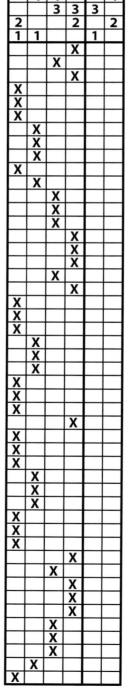

Threading
Border 1: 3 times
Alternate Motifs A and B: 5 times
Motif A: 1 time
Border 2: 3 times

Treadling
Motif: 1 time
Add tabby between each pattern thread.

Effervescence

This is such a complex-looking set of towels, but it is so worth taking the time to create. I chose to use Deep Royal Blue for the warp, contrasting with a White pattern thread, but any colors would be equally stunning. Instead of using 8/4 White for the pattern thread, use 8/2 for a softer look. Take your time in the threading process, breaking it down into smaller units and checking as you go. Before you know it, you will have finished it. Follow the same system when treadling. Breaking down the treadling motif into smaller units helps the weaver to maintain better control with fewer errors.

Begin your towel with 1.5 inches (3.8 cm) of plain weave, and then start the pattern following the sequence of Motifs. End with another 1.5 inches (3.8 cm) of plain weave. Next, weave 4 passes of a high-contrast thread, and then complete the second towel the same as the first. Finish each towel with a rolled hem.

Dimensions: 14.5 inches × 24 inches (36.8 × 61 cm)

Warp

Sett: 20 epi, 10 dent reed, 2 threads per dent
Length: 3-yard (2.7-m) warp
Thread: 8/2 Cotton Clouds Aurora Earth, Deep Royal Blue: 297 ends plus 2 floating selvedges = 299 ends, 900 yards (823 m)

Weft

Pattern thread: 8/4 cotton, White: 600 yards (548.6 m)
Tabby: 8/2 Cotton Clouds Aurora Earth, Deep Royal Blue: 700 yards (640.1 m)

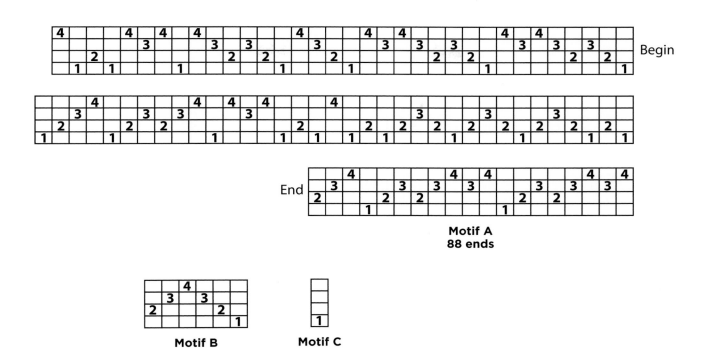

Begin

End

Motif A
88 ends

Motif B
6 ends

Motif C
1 end

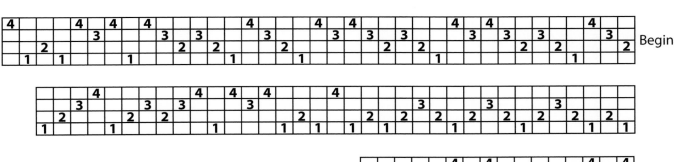

Begin

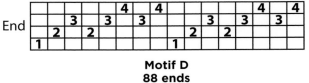

End

Motif D
88 ends

Threading
Motif A: 1 time
Motif B: 20 times
Motif C: 1 time
Motif D: 1 time

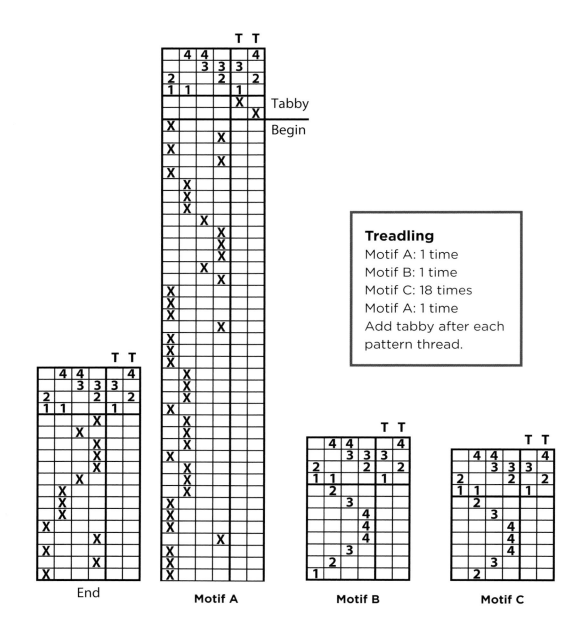

Treadling
Motif A: 1 time
Motif B: 1 time
Motif C: 18 times
Motif A: 1 time
Add tabby after each pattern thread.

Tabby
Begin

End

Motif A

Motif B

Motif C

Christmas Ornaments

A fun towel for the Christmas season! You've hung the ornaments on the tree; now you can hang some ornaments in your kitchen. Plan to take time weaving these towels. They won't weave up fast. There are lots of color changes, which will slow you down. One option that I often use is leaving a 3-inch thread hanging at the side; then, once the piece is off the loom, I hand weave these threads back into the piece. That allows me to keep weaving and also eliminates any buildup of threads along the edge.

Begin with 2 inches (5.1 cm) of plain weave in White followed by the 4 Green–4 Red–4 Green pattern also in plain weave. Now you are ready to start the ornament block. Put in 5 or 6 passes of White tabby, and then begin the ornament. If your ornaments are all standing in one direction, it will make no difference if you begin to read the treadling from the top or bottom. If you want them to mirror each other, you will need to reverse your treadling sequence. Finish with the 4 Green–4 Red–4 Green plain weave pattern. There are five repeats of the Christmas ornaments. Finish with 2 inches (5.08 cm) of plain weave. Weave a spacer between the towels with a high-contrast color, and then weave the second towel. Finish your towels with hems. Just a note: If you don't have Gold rug warp, use a double strand of 5/2 Gold perle cotton or a double strand of 8/2 Gold cotton. Have fun with these ornaments!

Dimensions: 15 inches × 22 inches (38.1 × 55.9 cm)

Warp
Sett: 20 epi, 10 dent reed, 2 threads per dent
Length: 3-yard (2.7-m) warp
Threads: 8/2 Cotton Clouds Aurora Earth
- White: 240 ends, 750 yards (685.8 m)
- Red: 20 ends, 75 yards (68.6 m)
- Kelly Green: 40 ends, 135 yards (123.4 m)

Weft
Cotton Clouds
Horizontal Stripes:
- 8/2 Red: 25 yards (22.9 m)
- 8/2 Kelly Green: 50 yards (45.7 m)

Motifs:
- 8/4 cotton Red: 75 yards (59.4 m)
- 8/4 cotton Green: 75 yards (59.4 m)
- 8/4 cotton Gold: 40 yards (36.6 m)

Tabby: 8/2 White: 500 yards (457.2 m)

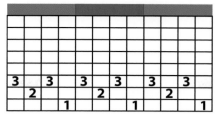

Threading
Alternate Motifs A
and B: 4 times
Motif A: 1 time

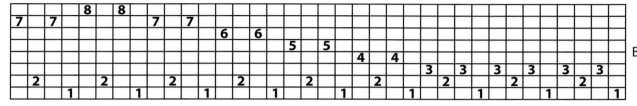

Motif A
12 ends

Motif B
60 ends
White

Begin

End

Tie-up and Treadling

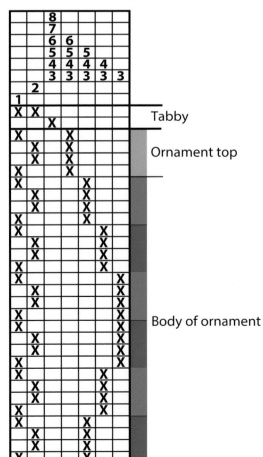

Tabby

Ornament top

Body of ornament

Treadling
Refer to text on page 85
for more information.
Insert tabby between
each pattern thread.

Star Journey

This set of towels will really make a statement in your kitchen. There are four stars, one in each corner, that anchor the pattern. Be sure to turn the towels over, as the reverse is just as attractive. The warp for these towels is the same, but the color of the pattern thread has changed. This is a benefit of a neutral warp—it allows you to choose and change your color.

Begin your towel with 1.5 inches (3.8 cm) of White tabby. Complete the treadling pattern as indicated just one time. Follow this step with another 1.5 inches (3.8 cm) of White tabby. Next, weave four passes with a high-contrast thread color to separate your towels. Now you are ready to weave the second towel just as you did the first one. Finish each towel with a rolled hem. Be sure to use a tabby thread after each pattern thread.

For variety, you might try using two colors in the warp. Use one color for the stars and another color for the center panel. Then you could bring in a different color for the pattern thread. Make these your own!

Dimensions: 14.5 inches × 23 inches (36.8 × 58.4 cm)

Warp

Sett: 20 epi, 10 dent reed, 2 threads per dent
Length: 3-yard (2.7-m) warp
Thread: 8/2 Cotton Clouds Aurora Earth, White: 289 ends plus 2 floating selvedges = 291 ends, 900 yards (823 m)

Weft

Pattern Threads: 8/4 Cotton Clouds
• Cranberry: 150 yards (137.2 m)
• Myrtle Green: 150 yards (137.2 m)
Tabby: 8/2 Cotton Clouds Aurora Earth, White: 400 yards (365.8 m)

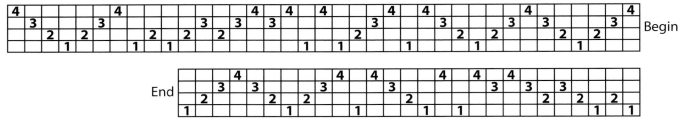

Begin

End

Motif A
64 ends

Threading
Motif A: 1 time
Motif B: 39 times
Motif C: 1 time
Motif D: 1 time

Motif B
4 ends

Motif C
5 ends

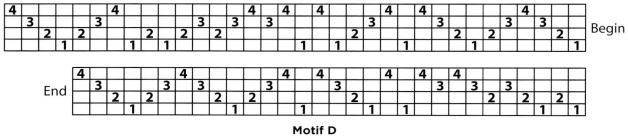

Begin

End

Motif D
64 ends

Tie-up and Treadling

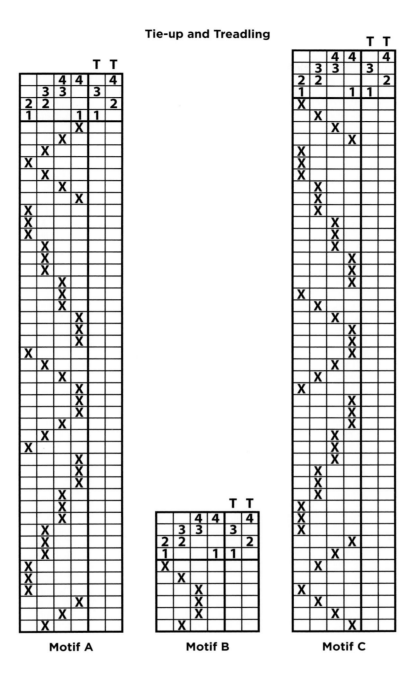

Motif A   Motif B   Motif C

Treadling

Motif A: 1 time
Motif B: 30 times
Motif C: 1 time
Add tabby thread after
each pattern thread.

Merry Christmas Towels

This is the perfect set of towels for the holidays and so very simple to weave! A simple threading of 1, 2, 3, 4 could not be easier. When I wind the warp for a project like this one, I wind each color as I go so that I know I have the threads in the correct order. It may be a bit slower, but I find that I'm less likely to make mistakes.

The treadling is equally simple: 1, 2, 3, 4. Just follow the same color sequence as in the threading. There is a lot of color change, so, to prevent buildup along the selvedge, I cut the thread, leaving approximately 3 inches (7.6 cm). Then, once the piece is off the loom, I use a needle and hand weave the tails back in. It's really very simple and takes no more time than fussing at the loom. Weave 2 inches (5.1 cm) of White in the twill pattern at the beginning of the towel. Repeat the motif 5 times per towel, ending with 2 Green threads to balance. Follow this with another 2 inches (5.1 cm) of twill in White. Weave four passes of a high-contrast thread for a spacer, and then repeat the sequence for the second towel. Finish your towels with a rolled hem.

Feel free to change the colors to fit your décor or any season!

Dimensions: 14.5 inches × 23 inches (36.8 × 58.4 cm)

Warp

Sett: 20 epi, 10 dent reed, 2 threads per dent
Length: 3-yard (2.7-m) warp
Threads: 8/2 Cotton Clouds Aurora Earth
- Dark Red: 72 ends, 235 yards (214.9 m)
- Kelly Green: 80 ends plus 2 floating selvedges = 82 ends, 275 yards (251.5 m)
- White: 138 ends, 450 yards (411.5 m)

Weft

8/2 Cotton Clouds Aurora Earth
- Dark Red: 125 yards (114.3 m)
- Kelly Green: 125 yards (114.3 m)
- White: 240 yards (219.5 m)

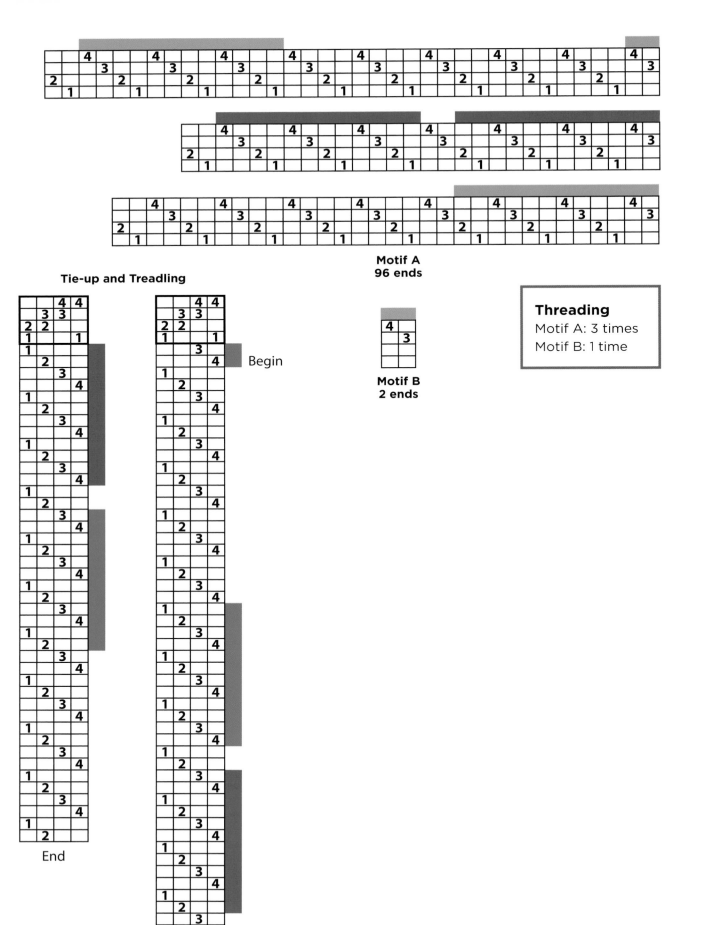

Tie-up and Treadling

Motif A
96 ends

Motif B
2 ends

Begin

End

Threading
Motif A: 3 times
Motif B: 1 time

Spring and Fall

Spring is such a beautiful time of year and a promise of warmer weather after the cold, cold winter. All the flowers bloom in soft colors, which are a part of this set of towels. Fall is equally beautiful with a different set of colors. This set of towels was perfect to showcase both seasons. The threading and treadling are, oh, so easy.

Note that the first treadle is repeated four times in a row. This arrangement makes the floating selvedge essential for this project. Because there were so many color changes, I cut the weft threads and left long ends that I hand wove back in after the towels were off the loom. The Natural/White thread is carried along the edge as you weave. Begin by weaving 1.5 inches (3.8 cm) of plain weave in either White or Natural. Then repeat the pattern 14 times followed with another 1.5 inches (3.8 cm) of plain weave. Weave four passes of a high-contrast thread to separate the towels, and then repeat the process for your second towel. Finish each towel with a rolled hem.

The draft is rather unusual, but it comes from the "Weaving Multiple Structures on an 8-Shaft Threading" class by Tom Knisely. Setting up your loom in this manner makes the threading and treadling very easy.

Dimensions: 15 inches × 25 inches (38.1 × 63.5 cm)
Sett: 20 epi, 10 dent reed, 2 threads per dent
Length: 3-yard (3-m) warp

SPRING

Warp

Threads: 8/2 Cotton Clouds Aurora Earth
- White: 114 ends plus 2 floating selvedges = 116 ends, 350 yards (320 m)
- Nile Green: 50 ends, 150 yards (137.2 m)
- Special Pink: 45 ends, 150 yards (137.2 m)
- Yellow: 45 ends, 150 yards (137.2 m)
- Baby Blue: 45 ends, 150 yards (137.2 m)

Weft

8/2 Cotton Clouds Aurora Earth
- White: 200 yards (182.9 m)
- Nile Green: 75 yards (68.6 m)
- Special Pink: 75 yards (68.6 m)
- Baby Blue: 75 yards (68.6 m)
- Yellow: 75 yards (68.6 m)

FALL

Warp

Threads: 8/2 Cotton Clouds Aurora Earth
- Natural: 114 ends plus 2 floating selvedges = 116 ends, 350 yards (320 m)
- Rust: 50 ends, 150 yards (137.2 m)
- Mustard: 45 ends, 150 yards (137.2 m)
- Light Brown: 45 ends, 150 yards (137.2 m)
- Chocolate: 45 ends, 150 yards (137.2 m)

Weft

8/2 Cotton Clouds Aurora Earth
- Natural: 200 yards (182.9. m)
- Rust: 75 yards (68.6 m)
- Light Brown: 75 yards (68.6 m)
- Mustard: 75 yards (68.6 m)
- Chocolate: 75 yards (68.6 m)

Threading and Color Sequence (Spring and Fall) — 32 ends

Color sequence (each repeat = 8 ends, stairstep shafts 8→1):

Color band	Chocolate	Natural/White	Mustard	Natural/White	Light Brown	Natural/White	Rust	Natural/White

Threading stairstep (repeated 4 times across the 32 ends):

Shaft	Ends
8	1, 9, 17, 25
7	2, 10, 18, 26
6	3, 11, 19, 27
5	4, 12, 20, 28
4	5, 13, 21, 29
3	6, 14, 22, 30
2	7, 15, 23, 31
1	8, 16, 24, 32

Threading and Color Sequence
(Spring and Fall)
32 ends

Threading (Spring and Fall)

Full Motif: 9 times
Partial Motif: 1 time

Partial Motif (Spring and Fall) — 11 ends

Color bands: Natural/White | Rust | Natural/White

End	1	2	3	4	5	6	7	8	9	10	11
Shaft	3	2	1	8	7	6	5	4	3	2	1

Partial Motif
(Spring and Fall)
11 ends

Tie-up and Treadling

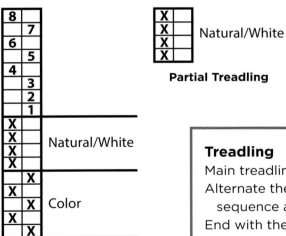

Tie-up: diagonal on shafts 8, 7, 6, 5, 4, 3, 2, 1.

Treadling:
- X X X X — Natural/White
- X X X X — Color

Partial Treadling

- X
- X
- X
- X — Natural/White

Treadling

Main treadling: 14 times
Alternate the colors in the same sequence as in the threading.
End with the Partial Treadling to balance.

Fruit
Cocktail

Weaving can be full of surprises! I designed this piece based on one side of the towels, the bright orange side. I loved the design that was created. But, once off the loom, I was pleasantly surprised by the reverse side. What a quandary! I'm not sure which side I like the best! So when I hemmed these towels, I hemmed one of each set on the opposite side so that I had one of each as the *right* side. This is a pattern that I think deserves some more investigation to see what other patterns might emerge with some small changes. You should also notice that it is an unusual draft. This was the result of a wonderful class with Tom Knisely about multiple patterns with a straight 8 threading.

The orange, yellow, and green are the bright colors of citrus fruits, which will really brighten your kitchen. Then I decided to do another colorway in purple, green, and lavender. So now we have a fruit salad with oranges, lemons, limes, plums, and green and purple grapes! Both sets of towels are just lovely, but, oh, how using different colors really changes the overall look.

Weave your first towel to 29 inches (73.7 cm). No special hem needed! Then weave four passes of a high-contrast thread to separate the towels. Weave the second towel to 29 inches (73.7 cm). Finish your towels with a rolled hem.

Dimensions: 14.5 inches × 27 inches (36.8 × 68.6 cm)
Sett: 20 epi, 10 dent reed, 2 threads per dent
Length: 3-yard (2.7-m) warp

ORANGE/GREEN/MAIZE COLORWAY

Warp

8/2 Cotton Clouds Aurora Earth
- Maize: 152 ends plus 2 floating selvedges = 154 ends, 475 yards (434.3 m)
- Kelly Green: 144 ends, 475 yards (434.3 m)

Weft

8/2 Cotton Clouds Aurora Earth, Orange: 525 yards (480.1 m)

GREEN/GRAPE/LAVENDER COLORWAY

Warp

8/2 Cotton Clouds Aurora Earth
- Nile Green: 152 ends plus 2 floating selvedges = 154 ends, 475 yards (434.3 m)
- Grape: 144 ends, 475 yards (434.3 m)

Weft

8/2 Cotton Clouds Aurora Earth, Lavender: 525 yards (480.1 m)

8								8							
	7								7						
		6								6					
			5								5				
				4								4			
					3								3		
						2								2	
							1								1

Yellow/Green Threading
16 ends

8							
	7						
		6					
			5				
				4			
					3		
						2	
							1

Yellow/Green Partial Block
8 ends

8								8							
	7								7						
		6								6					
			5								5				
				4								4			
					3								3		
						2								2	
							1								1

Green/Grape Threading
16 ends

Threading (Both Colorways)
Main Threading: 18 times
Partial Block: 1 time

8							
	7						
		6					
			5				
				4			
					3		
						2	
							1

Green/Grape Partial Block
8 ends

Tie-up and Treadling

	8		8
7		7	
	6		6
5		5	
			4
		3	
	2		
1			
			X
		X	
	X		
X			

Waves

I love a neutral warp! This approach gives the weaver so many options for color. In this set, the warp was Natural color cotton, giving the weaver the opportunity to weave towels of different colors. These towels are a crackle weave structure. You will have a pattern thread, which is the 8/4 rug warp. This is where your color will come in. After each pattern thread, you will throw a tabby thread. This addition gives the piece integrity! Without the tabby, the towels would be too floppy and the pattern blocks would be distorted.

The pattern is very simple to weave and yet creates such an optical effect. If you have a computer program, you could try different treadling patterns and find something different. This is the perfect draft to put on a long warp and have a huge variety of towels. If you want to increase to four towels, make your warp 5 yards (4.6 m). That should be very generous.

Begin your towel with 1.5 inches (3.8 cm) of plain weave. Repeat the treadling sequence two times, ending with the partial for balance. Next, weave another 1.5 inches (3.8 cm) of plain weave. Weave four passes of a high-contrast thread to separate the towels and repeat the entire sequence for the second towel. Finish each towel with rolled hems.

Dimensions: 15.5 inches × 23 inches (39.4 × 58.4 cm)

Warp
Sett: 20 epi, 10 dent reed, 2 threads per dent
Length: 3-yard (2.7-m) warp
Thread: 8/2 Cotton Clouds Aurora Earth,
   Natural: 289 ends plus 2 floating selvedges =
   291 ends, 900 yards (823 m)

Weft
Pattern threads: 8/4 cotton
 • Forest Green: 200 yards (182.9 m)
 • Cranberry: 200 yards (182.9 m)
Tabby: 8/2 Cotton Clouds Aurora Earth,
   Natural: 450 yards (411.5 m)

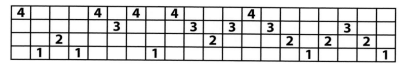

Motif A
20 ends

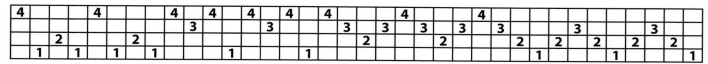

Motif B
36 ends

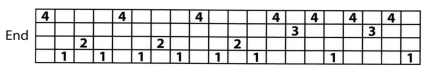

Begin

End

Motif C
52 ends

Border 1
2 times = 8 ends

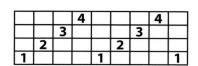

Border 2
1 time = 9 ends

Threading
Border 1: 2 times
Motifs A, B, and C: 2 times
Motifs A and B: 1 time
Border 2: 1 time

Tie-up

Treadling
A–D treadling sequence: 2 times
End with A for balance.
Use tabby between each pattern row.

A

B

C

D

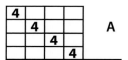

A

Treadling

Evergreen

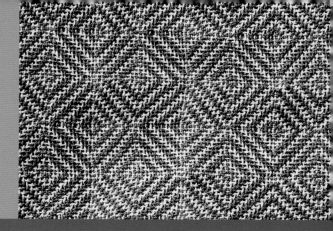

Diamonds within diamonds within diamonds! I love the way shadow weave takes a simple shape and makes a statement with it. While I chose two shades of green, you could use any color combination as long as it has a high contrast. Just be very careful in threading, as it is easy to mix up the threads. So be sure to take your time!

Also take care when treadling, being sure to treadle in the correct order with the correct color. Note that the treadling is to be read from the bottom up for this chart. This approach places the threads correctly for the pattern. You will have to do the partial motif only one time at the end.

There is a tabby in the tie-up, which is used at the beginning and end of each towel when weaving 1.5 inches (3.8 cm). Don't be alarmed—this is not a true tabby. However, it will give you a good area to create a rolled hem. Repeat the Full Motif 10 times, ending with the Partial Motif one time. Then weave another 1.5 inches (3.8 cm) of the faux tabby. Weave four passes of a high-contrast color to separate the towels, and then repeat the process for the second towel. I used the Nile Green for one towel tabby and the Green for the other towel tabby. This choice evens out the use of the colors. Finish each towel with a rolled hem.

Dimensions: 14.5 inches × 24 inches (36.8 × 61 cm)

Warp
Sett: 20 epi, 10 dent reed, 2 threads per dent
Length: 3-yard (2.7-m) warp
Threads: 8/2 Cotton Clouds Aurora Earth
- Nile Green: 146 ends plus 1 floating selvedge = 147 ends, 450 yards (411.5 m)
- Green: 146 ends plus 1 floating selvedge = 147 ends, 450 yards (411.5 m)

Weft
8/2 Cotton Clouds Aurora Earth
- Nile Green: 275 yards (251.5 m)
- Green: 275 yards (251.5 m)

Threading

Border: 1 time
Full Motif: 6 times
Border: 1 time

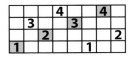

Border
8 ends

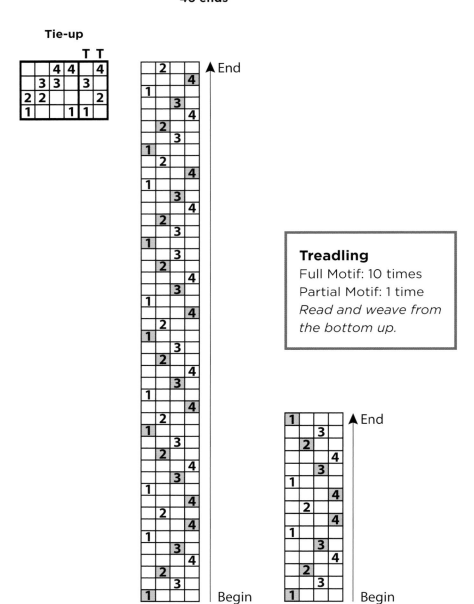

Full Motif
46 ends

Tie-up

Treadling

Full Motif: 10 times
Partial Motif: 1 time
*Read and weave from
the bottom up.*

Full Motif

Partial Motif

Lavender Blue Dilly Dilly

This set of towels has both color and pattern! The threading and tie up are based on M's & W's, which you can see when you study the threading. How fun is that! Lavender and Baby Blue are the perfect color combination. This would be a great set of towels for the half bath that visitors use. Just be careful, as they will want their own set.

Begin each towel with 1.5 inches (3.8 cm) of tabby in White. Starting with Motif A in Lavender, repeat Motifs A–D eight times following the color sequence. You will end with Motif A in Lavender. Then weave another 1.5 inches (3.8 cm) of tabby in White. Weave three or four passes of a high-contrast thread to separate your towels, and repeat the same process for the second towel. Finally, finish each towel with a rolled hem. Change up the colors to match your room and enjoy!

Dimensions: 15 inches × 24 inches (38.1 × 61 cm)

Warp
Sett: 20 epi, 10 dent reed, 2 threads per dent
Length: 3-yard (2.7-m) warp
Threads: 8/2 Cotton Clouds Aurora Earth
- Baby Blue: 91 plus 2 floating selvedges = 93 ends, 290 yards (265.2 m)
- Lavender: 104 ends, 325 yards (297.2 m)
- White: 111 ends, 340 yards (310.9 m)

Weft
8/2 Cotton Clouds Aurora Earth
- Baby Blue: 200 yards (182.9 m)
- Lavender: 250 yards (228.6 m)
- White: 300 yards (274.3 m)

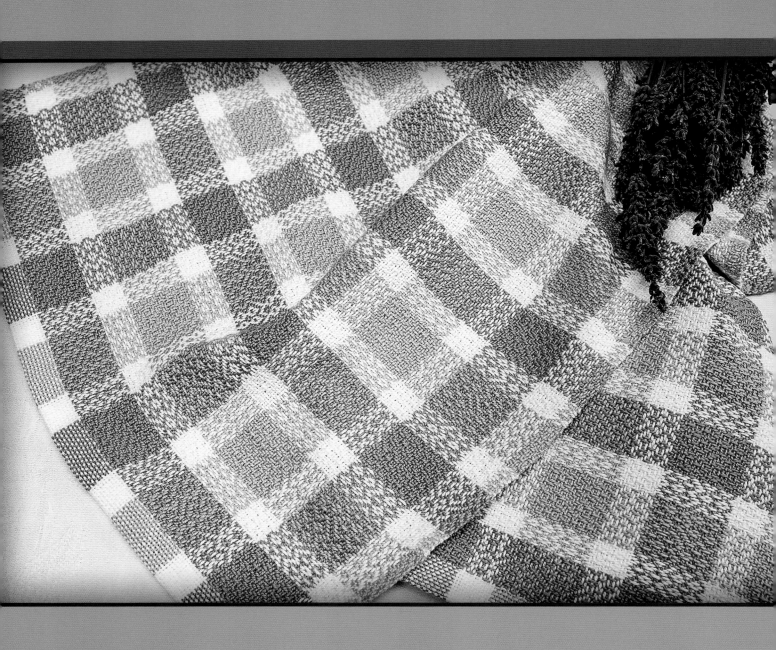

Threading
Border 1: 1 time
Alternate Motifs A,
 B, C, D: 3 times
Motif A: 1 time
Motif B: 1 time
Motif C: 1 time
Border 2: 1 time

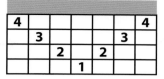

Border 1
7 ends

White

Motif A
13 ends

Motif B
26 ends

White

Motif C
13 ends

Motif D
26 ends

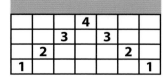

Border 2
7 ends

Treadling
Alternate Motifs A, B, C, D: 8 times
Motif A: 1 time

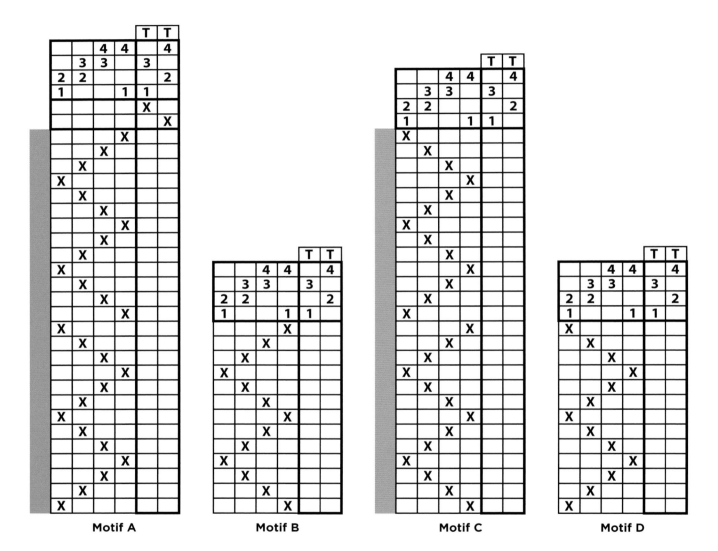

Motif A   Motif B   Motif C   Motif D

Fireworks

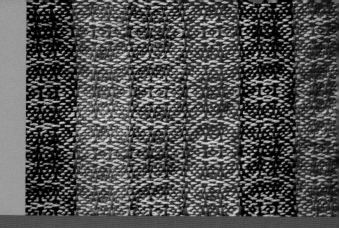

What could be more fun in the summer than to see a fireworks display? We love to see the sky light up with all the shapes and colors. Reds, blues, greens, and so many more! This set of towels is a celebration of those events. And you have to admit, they will certainly brighten up any kitchen.

Each motif is 21 threads and one color. I alternated Blue–Orange–Green–Red, repeating that sequence three times. The last two blocks are Blue and Orange. Feel free to substitute colors or shift these around. Since these colors are so saturated, the use of White for the weft brightens the towels.

Begin your towel with 1.5 inches (3.8 cm) of plain weave. Then alternate Motif A and B ten times, ending with one more repeat of Motif A. Weave another 1.5 inches (3.8 cm) of plain weave. Weave four passes of a high-contrast color to separate your towels, and then weave the second towel. Finish each towel with a rolled hem.

Dimensions: 14.5 inches × 24.5 inches (36.8 × 62.2 cm)

Warp

Sett: 20 epi, 10 dent reed, 2 threads per dent

Length: 3-yard (2.7-m) warp

Threads: 8/2 Cotton Clouds Aurora Earth

- Deep Royal Blue: 84 ends plus 1 floating selvedge = 85 ends, 260 yards (205.7 m)
- Kelly Green: 63 ends, 200 yards (160 m)
- Orange: 84 ends plus 1 floating selvedge = 85 ends, 260 yards (205.7 m)
- Dark Red: 63 ends, 200 yards (160 m)

Weft

8/2 Cotton Clouds Aurora Earth, White: 525 yards (480.1 m)

							8						8							
						7		7				7		7						
					6				6		6				6					
				5						5						5				
			4														4			
		3																3		
	2																		2	
1																				1

Motif A
21 ends

8																				8
	7																		7	
		6																6		
			5														5			
				4						4						4				
					3				3		3				3					
						2		2				2		2						
							1						1							

Motif B
21 ends

Threading
Alternate Motifs A and B: 7 times
Color arrangement: Blue, Orange, Green, Red

		8	8			8	8
	7			7	7		7
6			6		6	6	
5		5		5		5	
	4		4		4		4
	3	3		3			3
2		2	2			2	
1	1			1	1		
X							
	X						
		X					
			X				
				X			
					X		
						X	
							X
						X	
					X		
				X			
					X		
						X	
							X
						X	
					X		
				X			
			X				
		X					
	X						
X							

Motif A

		8	8			8	8
	7			7	7		7
6			6		6	6	
5		5		5		5	
	4		4		4		4
	3	3		3			3
2		2	2			2	
1	1			1	1		
							X
						X	
					X		
				X			
			X				
		X					
	X						
X							
	X						
		X					
			X				
		X					
	X						
X							
	X						
		X					
			X				
				X			
					X		
						X	
							X

Motif B

Treadling
Alternate Motifs A and B: 10 times
Motif A: 1 time

Cotton Candy

The county fair: noises, smells, people, and the ever-present pink cotton candy! Oh, the memories! These are special memories that we all share. And how I love pink cotton candy, even at my age. The colors in this set of towels, which is shadow weave, remind me of this yummy treat.

If pink doesn't fit your décor, the colors are easy to change. Just make sure to use colors of high contrast so the shadow effect is recognizable. Begin your towel with 1.5 inches (3.8 cm) of plain weave. Alternating Motifs A and B, weave these ten times, ending with Motif A one time. Then weave another 1.5 inches (3.8 cm) of plain weave. Weave four passes of a high-contrast thread to separate the towels, and then repeat the sequence for the second towel. *A note here: Notice that you are to read the treadling from the bottom up.* This is just as you would see the motif appear when you weave. Finish each towel with a rolled hem.

Dimensions: 14.5 inches × 24 inches (36.8 × 61 cm)

Warp

Sett: 20 epi, 10 dent reed, 2 threads per dent
Length: 3-yard (2.7-m) warp
Threads: 8/2 Cotton Clouds Aurora Earth
- Special Pink: 144 ends, 450 yards (411.5 m)
- Rose Red: 147—includes 2 floating selvedge ends, 450 yards (411.5 m)

Weft

8/2 Cotton Clouds Aurora Earth
- Special Pink: 275 yards (251.5 m)
- Rose Red: 275 yards (251.5 m)

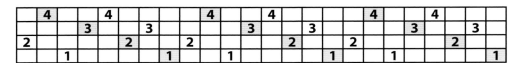

Border 1
24 ends

Motif A
21 ends

Motif B
23 ends

Border 2
24 ends

Tie-up

Threading
Border 1: 1 time
Alternate Motifs A
and B: 5 times
Motif A: 1 time
Border 2: 1 time

Treadling

Treadling
Alternate A and B:
10 times
Motif A: 1 time
Read and weave from the bottom up.

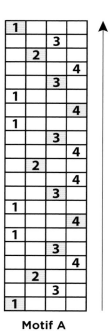

Motif A

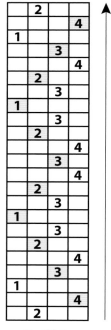

Motif B

Pretty Petite Pinwheels

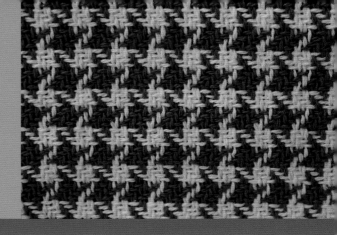

Pinwheels are always a favorite! And these tiny pinwheels are just perfect for a set of hand towels. The threading couldn't be easier, so this is a good draft for a novice weaver. You will need to be a bit careful with the treadling, but any mistake is very easy to spot right away. These towels could be made in any color combination. Change out the white weft for a color such as yellow or green. You will still see the pinwheels, but each towel will be unique.

This pattern is so small that it is not necessary to weave tabby for a special hem. Just weave the entire length of the towel: 28 inches (71.1 cm). Next, weave four passes of a high-contrast color to separate the towels, and then weave the second towel. Finish the towels with a rolled hem.

Dimensions: 15 inches × 24.5 inches (38.1 × 62.2 cm)

Warp

Sett: 20 epi, 10 dent reed, 2 threads per dent
Length: 3-yard (2.7-m) warp
8/2 Cotton Clouds Aurora Earth
- White: 148 ends, 475 yards (434.3 m)
- Jade: 152 ends plus 2 floating selvedges = 154 ends, 475 yards (434.3 m)

Weft

8/2 Cotton Clouds Aurora Earth
- White: 300 yards (274.3 m)
- Jade: 300 yards (274.3 m)

White

Full Motif
8 ends

4				4			
	3				3		
		2				2	
			1				1

Threading
Full Motif: 37 times
Partial Motif: 1 time

Partial Motif
4 ends

4			
	3		
		2	
			1

Tie-up and Treadling

4			4
3	3		
	2	2	
		1	1
X			
	X		
		X	
			X
	X		
X			
			X
		X	

White

Treadling
Repeat the motif, changing colors after each repeat.

Stripes and Diamonds

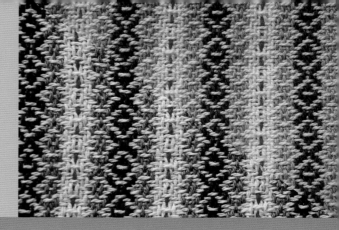

These sets of towels will take some time to thread due to all the color changes. But it will be worth the effort! Take your time when threading the heddles to prevent any mistakes. These towels will be perfect for the kitchen or guest bathroom. You will enjoy watching the diamonds form as you weave. Use your computer program and try some different treadling patterns. I'm sure you will find another pattern that is equally pleasing.

I've given you two different color combinations. In the threading draft, one is on top and the second under it. I'm sure you can come up with more colorways. Enjoy!

Weave your towel to 28–29 inches (71.1–73.7 cm). No need for a tabby with these towels. Then weave four passes of a high-contrast thread to separate the towels. Weave the second towel. Finish your towels with a rolled hem.

Dimensions: 15 inches × 24 inches (38.1 × 61 cm)
Sett: 20 epi, 10 dent reed, 2 threads per dent
Length: 3-yard (2.7-m) warp

BLUE/RED COLORWAY

Warp
Threads: 8/2 Cotton Clouds Aurora Earth
- Natural: 66 ends, 225 yards (205.7 m)
- Nassau Blue: 100 ends plus 2 floating selvedges = 102 ends, 325 yards (297.2 m)
- Empire Blue: 120 ends, 375 yards (342.9 m)
- Lipstick: 19 ends, 75 yards (68.6 m)

Weft
8/2 Cotton Clouds Aurora Earth, Natural: 550 yards (502.9 m)

GREEN/RED COLORWAY

Warp
Threads: 8/2 Cotton Clouds Aurora Earth
- White: 66 ends, 225 yards (205.7 m)
- Green: 100 ends plus 2 floating selvedges = 102 ends, 325 yards (297.2 m)
- Nile Green: 120 ends, 375 yards (342.9 m)
- Rose Red: 19 ends, 75 yards (68.6 m)

Weft
8/2 Cotton Clouds Aurora Earth, White: 550 yards (502.9 m)

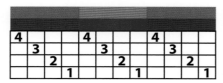

Border 1
12 ends

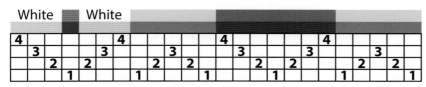

White   White

Motif
24 ends

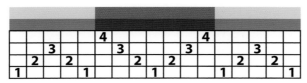

Partial Motif
17 ends

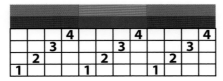

Border 2
12 ends

Threading

Border 1: 1 time
Motif: 11 times
Partial Motif: 1 time
Border 2: 1 time

Tie-up and Treadling

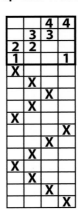

Broken Circles

This set of towels is destined for the guest bathroom. They are just too pretty to put in the kitchen and risk getting spaghetti sauce on them! The cotton variegated aquamarine warp is one of the softest fibers I've ever woven with. And, as often happens when working with variegated yarns, I had a surprise in the stripes that appeared in the warp. Those subtle stripes make a wonderful addition to the towels.

I love to play with the overshot patterns. For this set of towels, I used the Enigma overshot pattern but began with one half of the pattern, then the full pattern, and ended with one half of the pattern. Thus, the broken circles!

Begin each towel with 2 inches (5.1 cm) of plain weave, followed by one full repeat of the treadling pattern. Make sure to put a tabby thread after each pattern thread. Weave 8 inches (20.3 cm) of plain weave, and then one more repeat of the treadling pattern, ending with another 2 inches (5.1 cm) of plain weave. Weave four passes of a high-contrast thread to separate the towels, and weave the second towel in the same sequence. Finish your towels with a rolled hem.

Dimensions: 15 inches × 24.5 inches (38.1 × 62.2 cm)

Warp
Sett: 20 epi, 10 dent reed, 2 threads per dent
Length: 3-yard (2.7-m) warp
Thread: 8/2 Cotton Clouds, Aquamarine variegated: 301 ends plus 2 floating selvedges = 303 ends, 925 yards (845.8 m)

Weft
Cotton Clouds
8/2 Aquamarine variegated: 500 yards (457.2 m)
8/4 cotton, White: 200 yards (182.9 m)

Border 1
4 ends

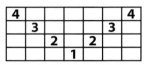

Begin

End

Motif A
43 ends

Threading
Border 1: 1 time
Alternate Motifs A
 and B: 5 times
Motif A: 1 time
Border 2: 1 time

Motif B
7 ends

Border 2
4 ends

Tie-up and Treadling

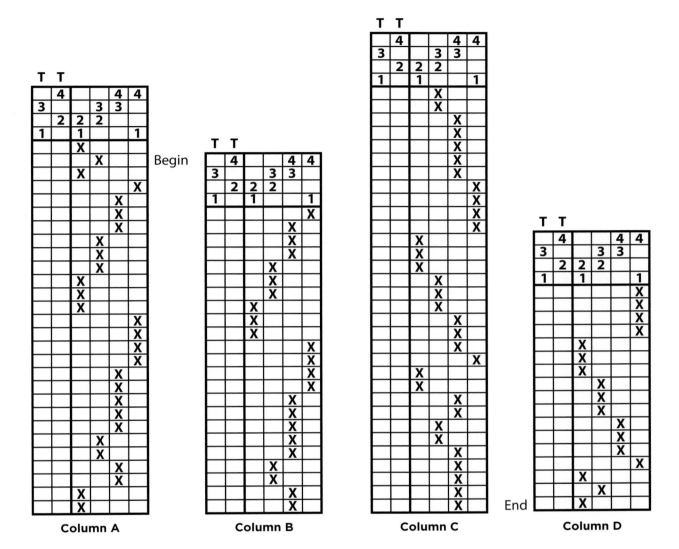

Begin

Column A

Column B

Column C

End

Column D

Treadling
Begin at top of Column A,
then Column B,
then Column C,
end at the bottom of Column D.
Repeat entire sequence 1 time.
Add tabby after each pattern thread.

Ghosts

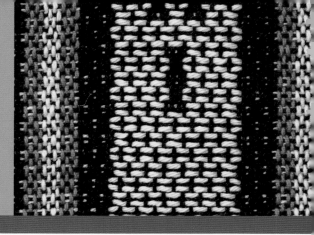

What a fun set of towels for the Halloween celebration! These would be perfect in the kitchen or guest bathroom. It would be easy to weave one long piece and have a table runner to match.

Begin and end each towel with 2 inches (5.1 cm) of plain weave in Black. Then weave the Orange/White/Orange horizontal stripes. Now you are ready to start the section with the ghosts. Weave eight passes of Black plain weave. You will also use Black for the tabby. There is a tabby thread after each pattern thread. Note the orientation of the ghosts. For the first set of ghosts, you will read the treadling from the bottom up. Follow this set with eight passes of plain weave in Black. Now you will alternate the Orange/White/Orange horizontal stripes with 2 inches (5.1 cm) of plain weave in Black. Do this 4 times.

For the next section of ghosts, you will read the treadling from the top down. Your ghosts will appear to be upside down as you are weaving. This is okay. Finish with one more repeat of the Orange/White/Orange stripes and then 2 inches (5.1 cm) of Black plain weave. You've finished the first towel! Weave four passes with a high-contrast color, and then repeat the process for the second towel. Finish each towel with a rolled hem. Enjoy!!!

Dimensions: 14.5 inches × 23 inches (36.8 × 58.4 cm)

Warp

Sett: 20 epi, 10 dent reed, 2 threads per dent

Length: 3-yard (2.7-m) warp

Threads: 8/2 Cotton Clouds Aurora Earth

- White: 24 ends, 75 yards (68.6 m)
- Black: 220 ends, 700 yards (640.1 m)
- Dark Orange: 48 ends plus 2 floating selvedges = 50 ends, 175 yards (160 m)

Weft

8/2 Cotton Clouds Aurora Earth

- White: 30 yards (27.4 m)
- Dark Orange: 60 yards (54.9 m)
- Black: 600 yards (548.6 m)

Pattern thread: 8/4 Cotton Clouds, White: 100 yards (91.4 m)

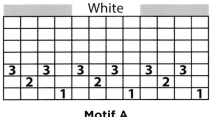

Motif A
12 ends

White

Begin

End

Motif B
44 ends

Threading

Alternate Motifs A and B: 5 times
Motif A: 1 time

Tie-up and Treadling

T T

Top of head

Eyes

Body

Mouth

Body
4X

Ruffled edge

T T

White

Treadling

See instructions in text
on page 129.
Add tabby after each
pattern thread.

Stair Steps

This set of towels can really play with your eyes. It looks like it might be difficult to weave but is really very simple. I chose to use purple and white for my color palette, but feel free to try something different. Just remember that a high contrast in color will give you a more well-defined pattern. And always be careful of using opposites on the color wheel. The results can be a very muddy color.

Begin your towel with 1.5 inches (3.8 cm) of plain weave with the White thread. To get the plain weave, you can use treadles 1 and 3 *or* 2 and 4. Then you can begin treadling the pattern. Repeat the treadling pattern eight times. If you want a longer towel, just repeat one pattern block. Weave another 1.5 inches (3.8 cm) of plain weave. Weave four passes of a high-contrast thread to separate your towels, and then repeat for the second towel. Finish each towel with rolled hems.

Dimensions: 14.5 inches × 24 inches (36.8 × 61 cm)

Warp

Sett: 20 epi, 10 dent reed, 2 threads per dent
Length: 3-yard (2.7-m) warp
Threads: 8/2 Cotton Clouds Aurora Earth
- Purple: 144 ends plus 1 floating selvedge = 145 ends, 450 yards (411.5 m)
- White: 144 ends plus 1 floating selvedge = 145 ends, 450 yards (411.5 m)

Weft

8/2 Cotton Clouds Aurora Earth
- Purple: 250 yards (228.6 m)
- White: 250 yards (228.6 m)

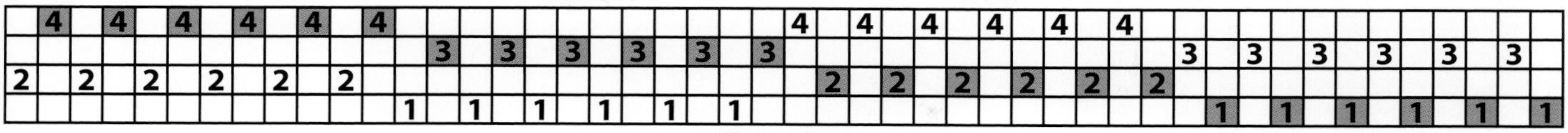

Threading
48 ends

Tie-up

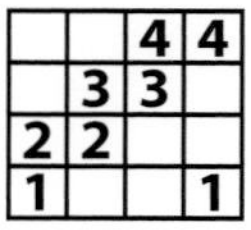

		4	4
	3	3	
2	2		
1			1

Threading
Thread sequence
6 times.

Treadling

Begin

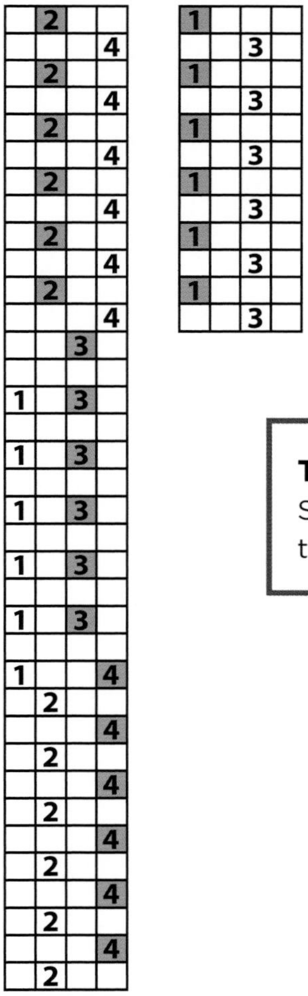

Treadling
See instructions in
text on page 131.

End

Prisms

Not only are these a stunning set of towels, but they are also a learning tool. Stand back and study the interaction of the colors in the tabby threads. You will find all varieties of colors formed with the interlacement of the fine threads. I used 12 different colors in the warp. Each motif is a separate color.

The colors from left to right: Yellow–Gold–Light Orange–Dark Orange–Special Pink–Beauty Rose–Dark Red–Nile Green–Kelly Green–Special Purple–Copen Blue–Nassau Blue.

You will be using a tabby after each pattern thread. I began with 1.5 inches (3.8 cm) of plain weave. For this project, I chose white, although you can use any color. The tabby changes with each motif, following the same sequence as the threading. You will go through one sequence of the colors for tabby and then reverse the colors back to the beginning. There are a total of 23 blocks.

Weave four passes of a high-contrast color to separate the towels, and then repeat the sequence for the second towel. Finish each towel with a rolled hem.

Have fun with this set of towels, and maybe save one as a color study.

Dimensions: 14.5 inches × 24.5 inches (36.8 × 62.2 cm)

Warp
Sett: 20 epi, 10 dent reed, 2 threads per dent
Length: 3-yard (2.7-m) warp
Threads: 8/2 Cotton Clouds Aurora Earth
- Nassau Blue: 24 ends plus 1 floating selvedge = 25 ends, 80 yards (73.2 m)
- Copen Blue: 24 ends, 80 yards (73.2 m)
- Special Purple: 24 ends, 80 yards (73.2 m)
- Kelly Green: 24 ends, 80 yards (73.2 m)
- Nile Green: 24 ends, 80 yards (73.2 m)
- Dark Red: 24 ends, 80 yards (73.2 m)
- Beauty Rose: 24 ends, 80 yards (73.2 m)
- Special Pink: 24 ends, 80 yards (73.2 m)
- Dark Orange: 24 ends, 80 yards (73.2 m)
- Light Orange: 24 ends, 80 yards (73.2 m)
- Gold: 24 ends, 80 yards (73.2 m)
- Yellow: 24 ends plus 1 floating selvedge = 25 ends, 80 yards (73.2 m)

Weft
Tabby: 8/2 Cotton Clouds Aurora Earth
- Each color: 25 yards (22.9 m)
- White: 60 yards (54.9 m)
Pattern Thread: 8/4 cotton, White: 300 yards (274.3 m)

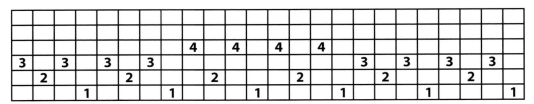

Motif A
24 ends

										4		4		4		4							
3		3		3		3											3		3		3		3
	2				2				2				2						2				2
			1				1				1				1				1				1

Motif B
24 ends

										6		6		6		6							
5		5		5		5											5		5		5		5
	2				2				2				2						2				2
			1				1				1				1				1				1

Tie-up and Treadling

T T

Tie-up:

	6	6	6				6	6
5	5	5	5	5				
4			4	4	4	4		
3				3	3	3	3	
2		2		2		2		2
1	1		1		1		1	

Treadling:

X									Tabby
	X								Tabby
		X						
			X					
		X						
			X					
				X				Motif A
					X			
				X				
					X			
		X						
			X					
		X						
			X					
						X		
							X	
						X		
							X	
								X	Motif B
								X
								X
						X		
							X	
						X		
							X	

Threading
Alternate Motifs A and B: 6 times
Follow colorway in description on page 135.

Treadling
Alternate Motifs A and B: 11 times
Motif A: 1 time
Add tabby.
Follow colorway in description on page 135.

Just a Box of Chocolates

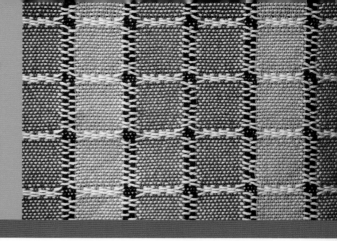

Chocolate! Next to ice cream, it's the best food ever. And when I looked through my fiber, those brown tones just screamed chocolate. The block formation created by this M's and O's weave structure was just perfect to accent the colors. We have luscious dark chocolate, creamy milk chocolate, white chocolate, and even cinnamon-covered bonbons. Just use your imagination.

The Chocolate (dark brown) is used for all the narrow stripes. The other three colors are used for the wider stripes, each stripe having 24 ends. My sequence for the three colors is: Chocolate–Light Brown–Chocolate–Mustard–Chocolate–Rust–Chocolate.

This sequence is repeated three times, although you can change the sequence if you choose. You will have the Chocolate (dark brown) on both edges. Be sure to include a floating selvedge. And be sure you catch that floater each time you pass the shuttle.

There is no traditional tabby, so I wove 1.5 inches (3.8 cm) alternating treadles 3 and 4. Next, repeat the full treadling motif 16 times, followed with another 1.5 inches (3.8 cm) alternating treadles 3 and 4. Weave four passes of a high-contrast thread to separate the towels, and repeat the process for your second towel. Finish each towel with a rolled hem.

Dimensions: 14.5 inches × 24 inches (36.8 × 61 cm)

Warp
Sett: 20 epi, 10 dent reed, 2 threads per dent
Length: 3-yard (2.7-m) warp
Threads: 8/2 Cotton Clouds Aurora Earth
- Chocolate: 80 ends plus 2 floating selvedges = 82 ends, 250 yards (228.6 m)
- Light Brown: 72 ends, 225 yards (205.7 m)
- Rust: 72 ends, 225 yards (205.7 m)
- Mustard: 72 ends, 225 yards (205.7 m)

Weft
8/4 cotton, Ivory: 400 yards (365.8 m)

Chocolate

Motif A
8 ends

				4		4	
3		3					
					2		2
	1		1				

Threading
Alternate Motifs A and B: 9 times
Motif A: 1 time

Color

Motif B
24 ends

4		4						4		4						4		4					
	3		3						3		3						3		3				
				2		2						2		2						2		2	
					1		1						1		1						1		1

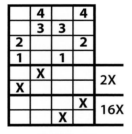

Full Motif

2X

16X

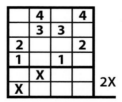

Partial Motif

2X

Treadling
Full Motif: 16 times
Partial Motif: 1 time

Barb's Flower Garden

have a friend who raises flowers. She has a yard full of perennials and then plants seeds and bulbs every spring. Walking through her garden is such a delight! It is full of color, bees, and butterflies! This set of towels is a tribute to her and all her work. The white threads in the warp and weft finish the illusion of a white picket fence surrounding the garden.

I used six different colors of 8/4 cotton for the flowers. You could change these colors or use just one color. If you don't have this many colors in 8/4 cotton, remember that you can use two strands of 8/2 cotton in its place. Just use two strands, but bear in mind that you will need twice as much yardage.

Begin your towel with 2 inches (5.1 cm) of plain weave using the Nile Green. Now you will begin your flower block, reading the chart from the bottom up. Weave four passes of White, followed by four passes of Nile Green, and then start the flower, using the Nile Green as your tabby. After you have completed your flower, weave another four passes of Nile Green. Then repeat the process, starting with the White until you have woven all six of your flowers. Balance with four passes of White and 2 inches (5.1 cm) of Nile Green plain weave. Weave four passes of a high-contrast color to separate your towels, and then weave the second towel. Finish your towels with a rolled hem. I hope you enjoy weaving these towels as much as I did creating them!

Dimensions: 15 inches × 23 inches (38.1 × 58.4 cm)

Warp

Sett: 20 epi, 10 dent reed, 2 threads per dent
Length: 3-yard (2.7-m) warp
Threads: 8/2 Cotton Clouds Aurora Earth
- Nile Green: 252 ends plus 2 floating selvedges = 254 ends, 800 yards (731.5 m)
- White: 40 ends, 150 yards (137.2 m)

Weft

8/2 Cotton Clouds Aurora Earth
- Nile Green: 300 yards (274.3 m)
- White: 30 yards (27.4 m)

8/4 Cotton from Cotton Clouds
- Myrtle Green: 100 yards (91.4 m)
- Royal Blue: 20 yards (18.3 m)
- Yellow: 20 yards (18.3 m)
- Orange: 20 yards (18.3 m)
- Red: 20 yards (18.3 m)
- Purple: 20 yards (18.3 m)

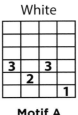

White

Motif A
4 ends

Threading
Motif A: 2 times
Alternate Motifs B and A: 7 times
Motif A: 1 time
Motif A is White. Motif B is Nile Green.

Motif B
36 ends

Tie-up and Treadling

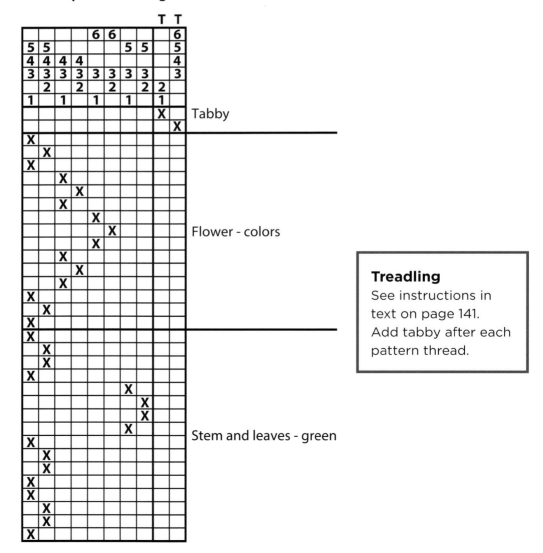

T T

Tabby

Flower - colors

Stem and leaves - green

Treadling
See instructions in
text on page 141.
Add tabby after each
pattern thread.

Perfect for Easter

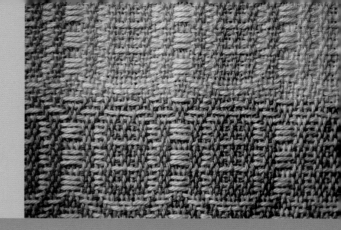

OK . . . maybe not *just* for Easter! But they are just the right colors to highlight a basket of Easter eggs that you have dyed with your children or grandchildren. Be sure to notice that you get more than five colors in the tabby areas. Where different colors cross, your eye blends these colors, making new colors.

The color placement is easy, and no, it doesn't necessarily follow the threading pattern exactly, but it works out beautifully. Don't overthink this! Below are the numbers of threads and colors.

- Lavender: 28 threads
- Yellow: 30 threads
- Baby Blue: 30 threads — Repeat this sequence two
- Special Pink: 30 threads   times for your warp
- Nile Green: 30 threads
- Lavender: 27 threads

Begin and end each towel with 1.5 inches (3.8 cm) of plain weave. It really makes no difference what color you use, but I chose to begin with Lavender. Using the 8/2 Lavender as the tabby thread, weave one treadling pattern. Then, following the color sequence, change the tabby thread for each subsequent treadling block. Weave 15 blocks ending with the partial threading to balance the final block. Finish with another 1.5 inches (3.8 cm) of plain weave. Weave four passes of a high-contrast thread to separate your towels, and then weave the second towel following the same sequence. Finish each towel with a rolled hem.

Dimensions: 14.75 inches × 24.5 inches (37.5 × 62.2 cm)

Warp
Sett: 20 epi, 10 dent reed, 2 threads per dent
Length: 3-yard (2.7-m) warp
Threads: 8/2 Cotton Clouds Aurora Earth
- Baby Blue: 60 ends, 200 yards (182.9 m)
- Nile Green: 60 ends, 200 yards (182.9 m)
- Special Pink: 60 ends, 200 yards (182.9 m)
- Yellow: 60 ends, 200 yards (182.9 m)
- Lavender: 55 ends plus 2 floating selvedges = 57 ends, 200 yards (182.9 m)

Weft
Tabby threads: 8/2 Cotton Clouds Aurora Earth
- Baby Blue: 100 yards (91.4 m)
- Nile Green: 100 yards (91.4 m)
- Special Pink: 100 yards (91.4 m)
- Yellow: 100 yards (91.4 m)
- Lavender: 150 yards (137.2 m)

Pattern thread: 8/4 cotton, White: 275 yards (251.5 m)

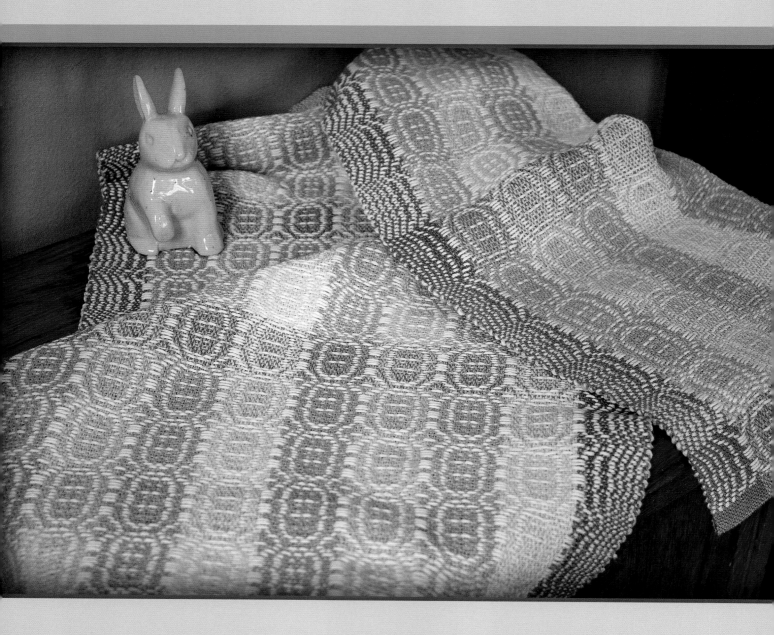

Threading

Border 1: 4 times
Motif A: 8 times
Motif B: 1 time
Border 2: 4 times

Border 1
4 ends

Border 2
4 ends

Motif A
30 ends

Motif B
25 ends

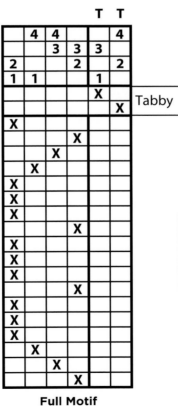

T   T

Tabby

Full Motif

Treadling

See instructions in text
on page 143.
Add tabby following
instructions for color.

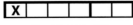

Partial Motif

Diamonds
Are Forever

Twills are always a favorite for the weaver. There are so many patterns, and they look so intricate that they can be intimidating. This is one of those twills—very impressive to look at; however, it is a very simple threading and treadling. Take advantage of this set of towels by putting on a warp for the two towels and maybe even four. If you do want to weave four towels, increase the warp to 5 yards (4.6 m). Then weave them all in different colors. What a beautiful set you will have! Perfect for your home or as a gift for that special someone.

Begin your towel with 1.5 inches (3.8 cm) of plain weave. Then alternate Motifs A and B nine times, and balance with one more repeat of Motif A. Weave another 1.5 inches (3.8 cm) of plain weave and then four passes of a high-contrast thread to separate the towels. Repeat the process for the second towel. Finish your towels with a rolled hem.

Dimensions: 14.75 inches × 24.5 (37.5 × 62.2 cm)

Warp
Sett: 20 epi, 10 dent reed, 2 threads per dent
Length: 3-yard (2.7-m) warp
Thread: 8/2 Cotton Clouds Aurora Earth, White: 295 ends plus 2 floating selvedges = 297 ends, 900 yards (823 m)

Weft
8/2 Cotton Clouds Aurora Earth
• Green: 275 yards (251.5 m)
• Empire Blue: 275 yards (251.5 m)

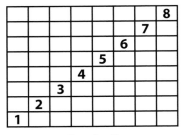

Border 1
8 ends

Motif A
15 ends

Motif B
29 ends

Border 2
8 ends

Threading
Border 1: 1 time
Alternate Motifs A
   and B: 6 times
Motif A: 1 time
Border 2: 1 time

Motif A

Motif B

Treadling
Alternate Motifs A and B
End with Motif A

Naturally Huck

This stunning set of towels is woven using soft organic cotton. This cotton has a wonderful hand and is very absorbent—perfect for either the kitchen or the guest bathroom. Once you have finished your set of towels, soak them in water mixed with baking soda. This process will brighten the natural colors. And the more they are used and washed, the darker the colors will become.

Begin the towel with 2.5 inches (6.4 cm) of plain weave. Then weave the Border one time. Alternate Motifs A and B six times and end with a Motif A. Balance your pattern with one more repeat of the Border and finally another 2.5 inches (6.4 cm) of plain weave. Weave four passes of a high-contrast color to separate your towels, and weave your second towel the same as the first. Finish your towels with a rolled hem.

Dimensions: 18 inches × 24 inches (45.7 × 61 cm)

Warp

Sett: 24 epi, 12 dent reed, 2 threads per dent
Length: 3-yard (2.7-m) warp
Threads: 10/2 Cotton Clouds American Maid Organic Cotton
- Natural: 136 ends, 425 yards (388.6 m)
- Light Green: 180 ends, 575 yards (525.8 m)
- Dark Green: 120 ends, 400 yards (365.8 m)

Weft

10/2 Cotton Clouds American Maid Organic Cotton, Natural: 800 yards (731.5 m)

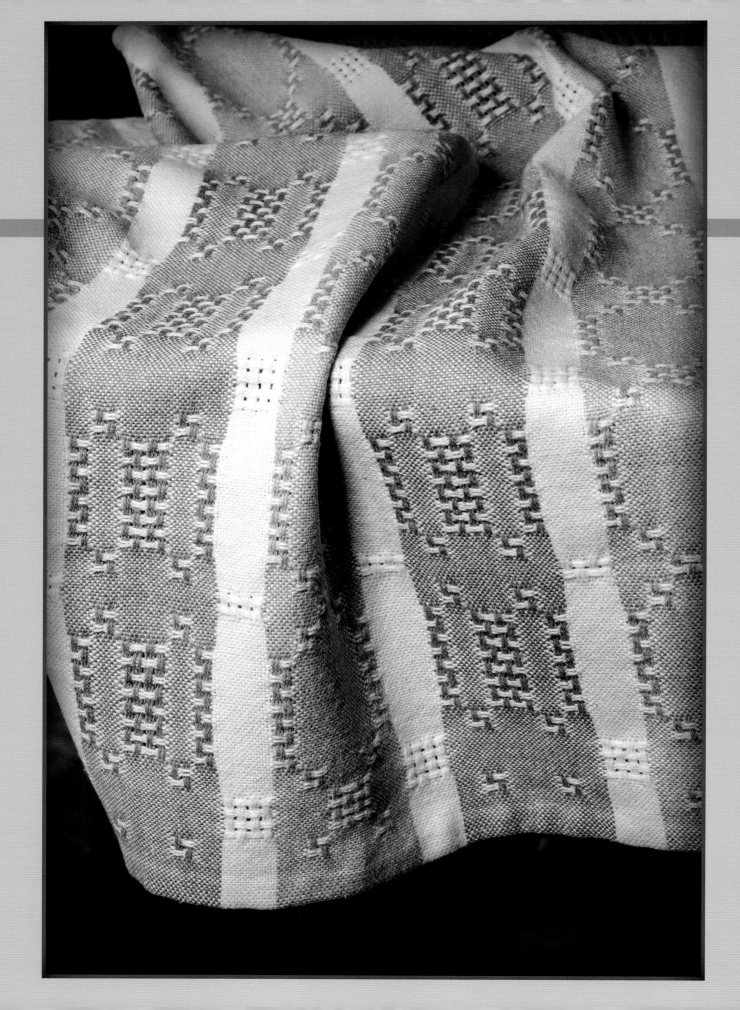

Begin

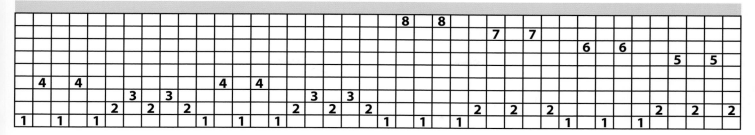

Natural

Border
2 ends

End

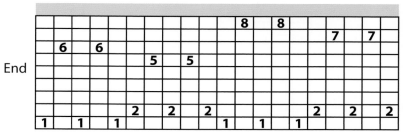

Motif A
60 ends

Natural

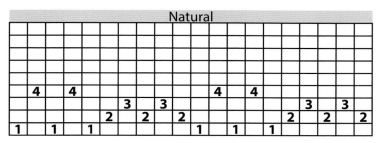

Motif B
20 ends

Begin

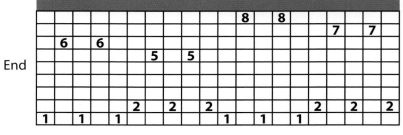

Threading

Border: 14 times

Alternate Motifs A, B, C, B:
   2 times

Motif A: 1 time

Border: 14 times

End

Motif C
60 ends

Tie-up and Treadling

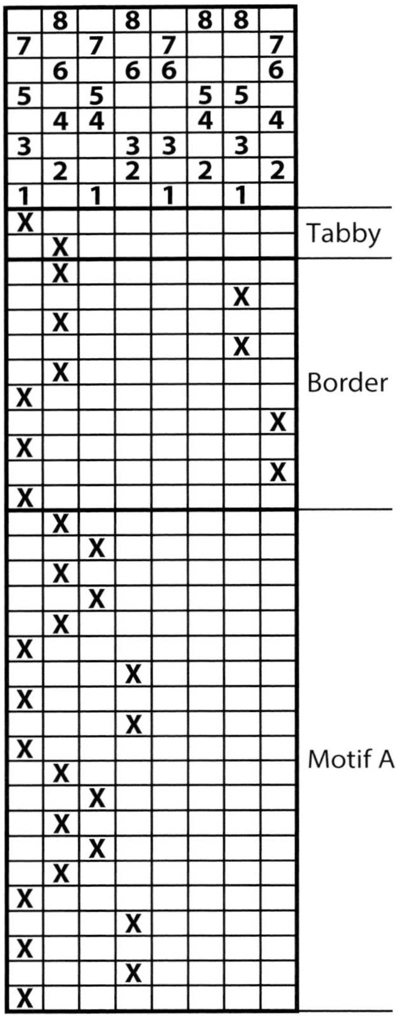

Tabby

Border

Motif A

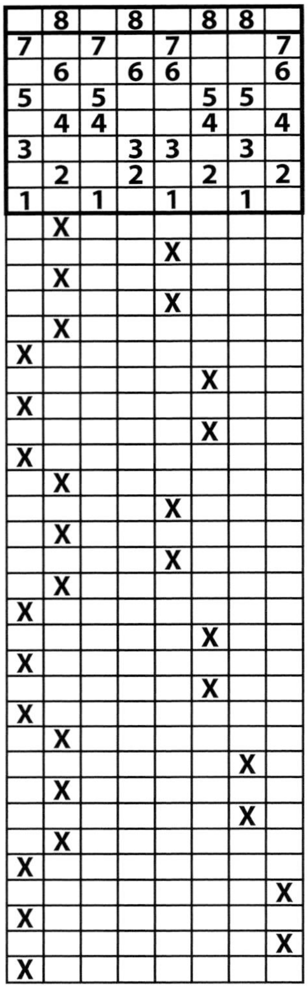

End

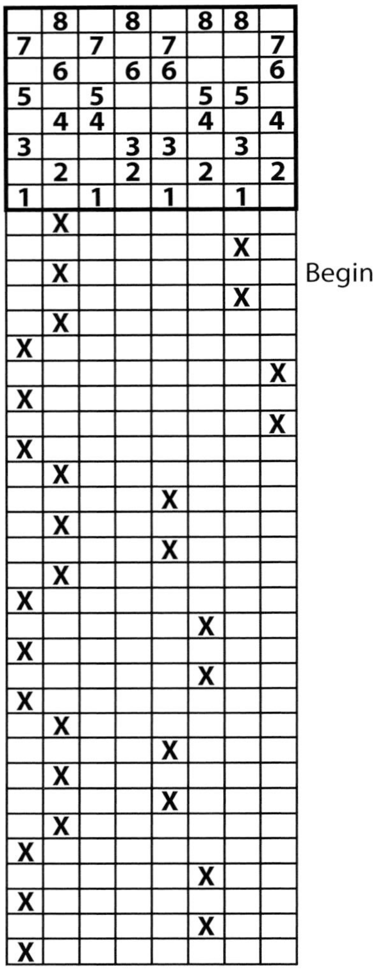

Begin

Motif B

Treadling
Border: 1 time
Alternate Motifs A and B: 6 times
Motif A: 1 time
Border: 1 time

152 | NATURALLY HUCK

Beautiful Borders

I t is important to remember that you do not have to weave a pattern over the entire towel. Using the pattern to create a border is a wonderful way to emphasize the beauty of the weave and still have a marvelous piece. These towels would be perfect for a guest bath or a gift. For the design to be prominent, the pattern thread will be larger than the warp thread, usually two times the size of the warp. After each pattern thread, you will insert a tabby thread. This addition stabilizes the pattern.

For the first towel, begin with 2.5 inches (6.4 cm) of plain weave. Next, you will begin with the Treadling 1 pattern. Repeat this pattern nine times and balance with the partial treadling. Then you will weave 14 inches (35.6 cm) of plain weave. Repeat the pattern, and finally weave another 2.5 inches (6.4 cm) of tabby.

Insert four passes of a high-contrast thread to separate the two towels. For the second towel, the process is the same. Weave 2.5 inches (6.4 cm) of plain weave. Then begin with Treadling 2 pattern. Repeat this pattern six times and balance with the partial treadling. Next, weave 14 inches (35.6 cm) of plain weave, and then repeat the pattern. End with 2.5 inches (6.4 cm) of plain weave. Finish both towels with rolled hems.

You will notice that this is a 6-shaft pattern. I added shafts 5 and 6 so that I could create a tabby along the edge, which gives the edges in the pattern area more stability. If you want to create these towels and have only 4 shafts, eliminate shafts 5 and 6 and the warp threads that go with them. You will just have to be careful in the pattern area to catch the floating selvedge.

Dimensions: 15 inches × 24 inches (38.1 × 61 cm)

Warp

Sett: 20 epi, 10 dent reed, 2 threads per dent

Length: 3-yard (2.7-m) warp

Thread: 8/2 Cotton Clouds Aurora Earth, White: 300 ends plus 2 floating selvedges = 302 ends, 925 yards (845.8 m)

Weft

Cotton Clouds

Tabby thread: 8/2 White: 600 yards (548.6 m)

Pattern threads:
- 8/4 Orange: 60 yards (54.9 m)
- 8/4 Purple: 50 yards (45.7 m)

Threading
Border: 1 time
Motif: 9 times
Border: 1 time

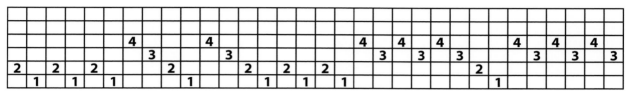

Border (optional)
6 ends

Motif
32 ends

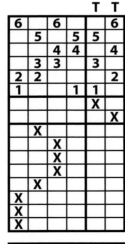

Treadling 1
See instructions in text on page 153.
Add tabby.

X
X
Final to Balance

Treadling 2
See instructions in text on page 153.
Add tabby.

X
Final to Balance

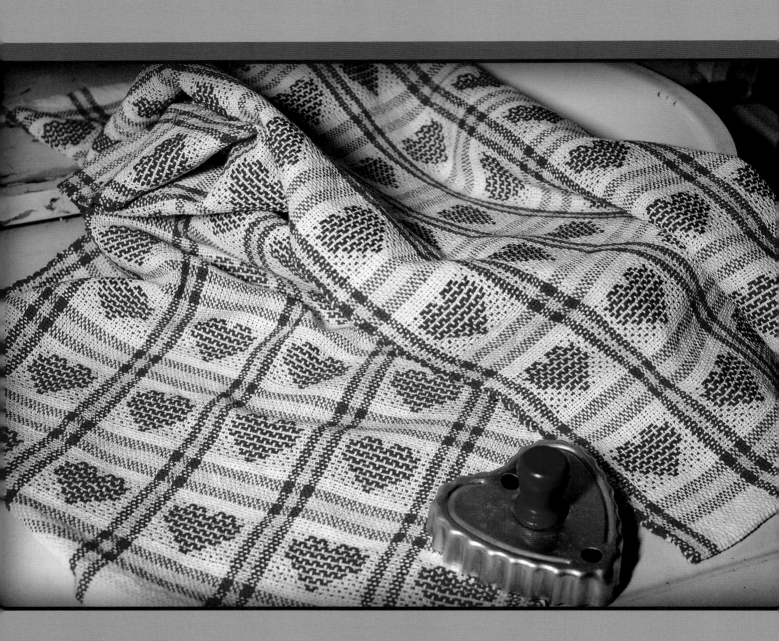

I Have a Heart for You

These are the perfect towels for Valentine's Day or a wedding/anniversary gift! Use different colors for the hearts, and they will look like candy hearts. This is a summer and winter tie-up, so substitute the appropriate blocks. There was a lot of un-weaving before the heart took shape. You will also see that there is some multi-treadling! Just take your time, and you will soon get a rhythm. You can treadle from the top down or bottom up and have hearts going in different directions on the same towel.

Begin with 1.5 inches (3.8 cm) of plain weave in White.

Step 1. Weave the following:
- Rose Red: 4 threads
- Special Pink: 4 threads
- Rose Red: 4 threads

Step 2. Weave the heart motif blocks. Begin with 4 threads of White, and then weave the heart followed with another 4 threads of White. Be sure to add the tabby after each pattern thread in the heart.

Repeat steps 1 and 2 nine times. Repeat step 1 a final time, and then weave 1.5 inches (3.8 cm) of plain weave.

Weave four passes of a high-contrast color to separate the towels, and repeat for the second towel. Finish your towels with a rolled hem.

Dimensions: 15 inches × 24 inches (38.1 × 61 cm)

Warp
Sett: 20 epi, 10 dent reed, 2 threads per dent
Length: 3-yard (2.7-m) warp
Threads: 8/2 Cotton Clouds Aurora Earth
- White: 216 ends, 700 yards (640.1 cm)
- Rose Red: 56 ends plus 2 floating selvedges = 58 ends, 200 yards (182.9 cm)
- Special Pink: 28 ends, 100 yards (91.4 cm)

Weft
8/2 Cotton Clouds Aurora Earth
- White: 500 yards (228.6 m)
- Rose Red: 50 yards (22 m)
- Special Pink: 30 yards (11 m)

Pattern thread: 8/4 Cotton Clouds, Red: 125 yards (114.3 m)

Threading

Alternate Motifs A
and B: 6 times
Motif A: 1 time

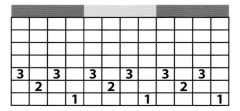

Motif A
12 ends

Motif B
36 ends

Treadling

See instructions in
text on page 157.
Add tabby after each
pattern thread.

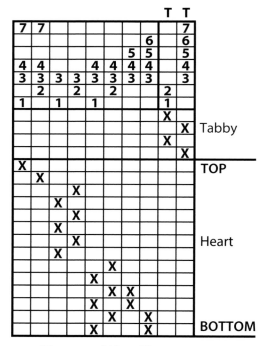

T T

Tabby

TOP

Heart

BOTTOM

Tie-up and Treadling

Razzleberry

These towels really make a statement with the small squares floating throughout the towel . . . and may mess with your eyes a bit! You can easily change the size of the squares by repeating that portion of the treadling pattern. And, of course, try a different color combination—just make sure you have a high-contrast light and dark thread.

Begin your towel with 1.5 inches (3.8 cm) of plain weave. Choosing either treadles 2 and 4 or treadles 1 and 3 will give you a plain weave. Next, begin the treadling pattern alternating Motifs A and B 16 times. End with one more repeat of Motif A. Weave another 1.5 inches (3.8 cm) of plain weave. Weave four passes of a high-contrast thread to separate your towels, and then weave the second towel. Finish your towels with a rolled hem. It is best to use a floating selvedge with this pattern so that the threads are caught consistently at the edge.

Dimensions: 15 inches × 23 inches (38.1 × 58.4 cm)

Warp
Sett: 20 epi, 10 dent reed, 2 threads per dent
Length: 3-yard (2.7-m) warp
Threads: 8/2 Cotton Clouds Aurora Earth
- Lipstick: 150 ends plus 1 floating selvedge = 151 ends, 475 yards (434.3 m)
- Yellow: 150 ends plus 1 floating selvedge = 151 ends, 475 yards (434.3 m)

or
- Black: 150 ends plus 1 floating selvedge = 151 ends, 475 yards (434.3 m)
- Silver: 150 ends plus 1 floating selvedge = 151 ends, 475 yards (434.3 m)

Weft
8/2 Cotton Clouds Aurora Earth
- Lipstick: 275 yards (251.5 cm)
- Yellow: 275 yards (251.5 cm)

or
- Black: 275 yards (251.5 cm)
- Silver: 275 yards (251.5 cm)

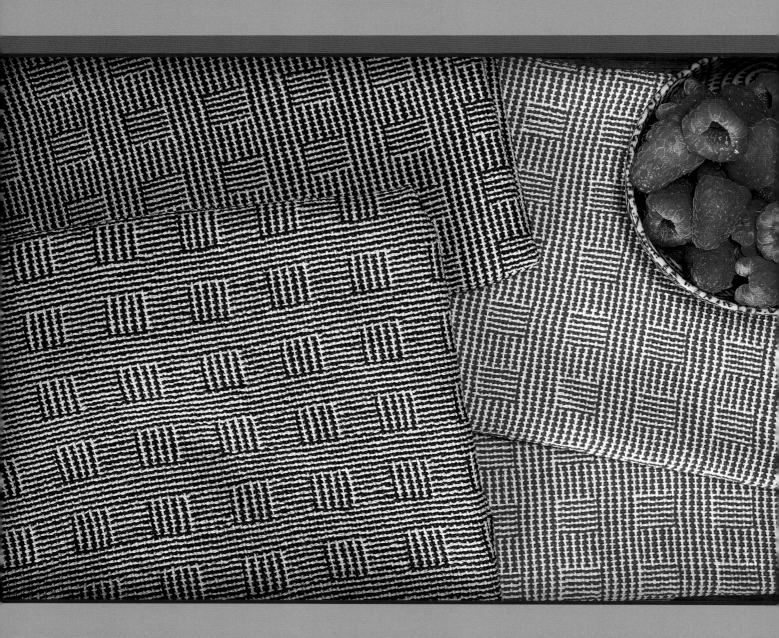

Motif A
12 ends

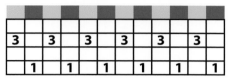

Motif B
12 ends

Threading
Alternate Motifs A
 and B: 12 times
Motif A: 1 time

Tie-up

		4	4
	3	3	
2	2		
1			1

Treadling

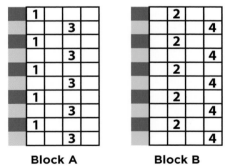

Block A   **Block B**

Treadling
See instructions
in text on page
159.

Diamonds and Lace

Weddings are so very special! These towels are just elegant enough for the perfect wedding gift! The diamonds are beautifully framed in wide bands of plain weave. The American Maid organic cotton is very soft and absorbent, which is perfect for towels. You might think about adapting this pattern for a baby blanket, especially if you live in a warm climate.

Begin each towel with 2.5 inches (6.4 cm) of plain weave. Then alternate Motifs A and B 7 times. Repeat Motif A one more time for balance. Finish with another 2.5 inches (6.4 cm) of plain weave. Weave four passes of a high-contrast color to separate your towels, and then weave the second towel. Finish each towel with a rolled hem.

The more you wash the organic cotton, the darker the colors will become. But you can give them a boost by soaking your towels in a mixture of water and baking soda.

Dimensions: 18 inches × 23 inches (45.7 × 58.4 cm)

Warp
Sett: 24 epi, 12 dent reed, 2 threads per dent
Length: 3-yard (2.7-m) warp
Thread: American Maid Organic Cotton, Dark Brown: 427 ends, 1,300 yards (1,188.7 m)

Weft
American Maid Organic Cotton, Natural: 800 yards (731.5 m)

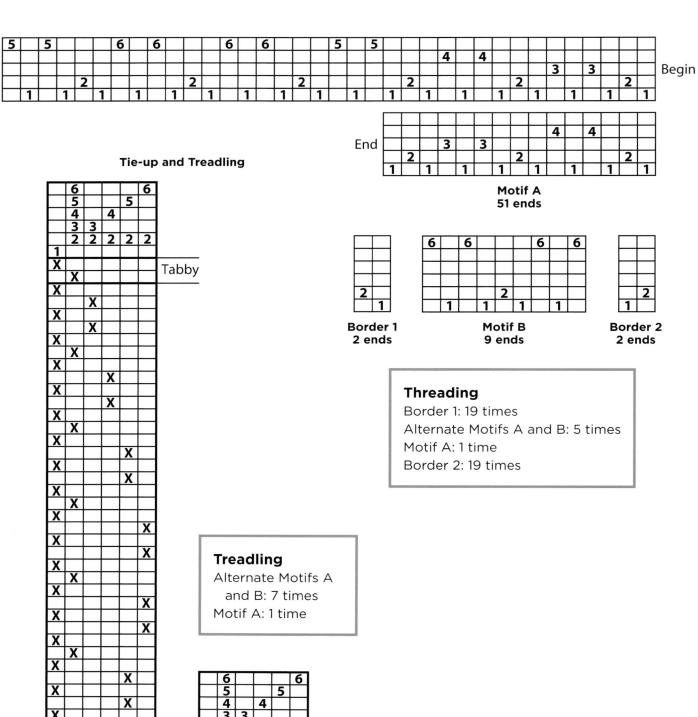

Tie-up and Treadling

Tabby

Motif A

Motif B

Begin

End

Motif A
51 ends

Border 1
2 ends

Motif B
9 ends

Border 2
2 ends

Threading
Border 1: 19 times
Alternate Motifs A and B: 5 times
Motif A: 1 time
Border 2: 19 times

Treadling
Alternate Motifs A
  and B: 7 times
Motif A: 1 time

Trio of Towels

A white warp is like a brand-new blank canvas for a painter. It offers so many options. As weavers, we love having a warp that will give us the chance to try different treadling patterns and use different colors. This set of towels gives you the chance to play! The threading is a very simple M's & W's threading, but the treadling changes! And if you have a computer weaving program, you may find many more options.

Color is another factor. By changing colors for each towel, you can use up some of those smaller amounts. You could even try weaving horizontal stripes for something really different.

Begin each towel with 1.5 inches (3.8 cm) of plain weave. You can use White or the same color as the pattern. Then weave your towel to length, approximately 26 inches (66 cm). Follow this with another 1.5 inches (3.8 cm) of plain weave. Now weave four passes of a high-contrast color to separate your towels. Repeat this process for each towel. Finish with a rolled hem.

You could easily weave more than three towels. I've given you a 3.5-yard (3.2-m) warp for completing three towels. For each additional towel, add another 30 inches (76.2 cm). Have fun!

Dimensions: 15 inches × 24 inches (38.1 × 61 cm)

Warp
Sett: 20 epi, 10 dent reed, 2 threads per dent
Length: 3.5-yard (3.2-m) warp
Thread: 8/2 Cotton Clouds Aurora Earth, White: 299 ends plus 2 floating selvedges = 301 ends, 1,150 yards (1,051.6 m)

Weft
8/2 Cotton Clouds Aurora Earth
- Empire Blue: 250 yards (228.6 m)
- Rose Red: 250 yards (228.6 m)
- Purple: 250 yards (228.6 m)

Border 1
4 ends

Motif A
11 ends

Motif B
11 ends

Border 2
4 ends

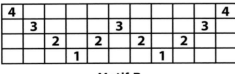

Threading
Border 1: 3 times
Alternate Motifs A
   and B: 12 times
Motif A: 1 time
Border 2: 3 times

Tie-up and Treadling

Full Motif — Tabby

Partial Motif

Rose Red Treadling
Repeat Full Motif to length, end with Partial Motif to balance.

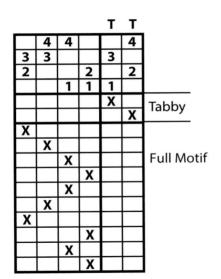

Tabby

Motif A

Motif B

Empire Blue Treadling
Alternate Motifs A and B to length, end with Motif A to balance.

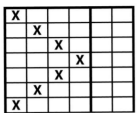

Tabby

Motif A

Motif B

Purple Treadling
Alternate Motifs A and B to length, end with Motif A to balance.

Sparklers Plus One

This pattern took me back to my childhood—July 4 with my family and a box full of fireworks! Of course, I was not allowed to handle the sparklers until I was older. Living in the country has its advantages. It would be very dark, since we didn't have any streetlights. This made the sparklers more fun. We would write our names, draw hearts, or just make swirls and curls. One look at this pattern, and I knew it would have to be the colors of the dark night sky and the gold sparklers.

This was such a fun and easy pattern I just couldn't resist making another set with Christmas colors. These will be wonderful for the holiday season. Do you have a Christmas potluck to attend? Take a set of these for your hostess. She will love them.

Blue/Gold

Begin with 1.5 inches (3.8 cm) of plain weave. Repeat the treadling sequence 19 times and then end with the Partial Motif. Follow this step with 1.5 inches (3.8 cm) of plain weave. Weave four passes of a high-contrast thread to separate the towels, and repeat the sequence for the second towel. Finish the towels with a rolled hem.

Red/Green/White

Begin with 1.5 inches (3.8 cm) of plain weave. Repeat the treadling sequence 14 times and end with the Partial Motif. Follow this with 1.5 inches (3.8 cm) of plain weave. Weave four passes of a high-contrast thread to separate the towels and repeat the sequence for the second towel. Finish the towels with a rolled hem.

Dimensions: 15 inches × 24.5 inches (38.1 × 62.2 cm)
Sett: 20 epi, 10 dent reed, 2 threads per dent
Length: 3-yard (2.7-m) warp

BLUE/GOLD

Warp
8/2 Cotton Clouds Aurora Earth
- Dark Blue: 156 ends plus 2 floating selvedges = 158 ends, 500 yards (457.2 m)
- Gold: 144 ends, 450 yards (411.5 m)

Weft
8/2 Cotton Clouds Aurora Earth
- Dark Blue: 250 yards (228.6 m)
- Gold: 250 yards (228.6 m)

PLUS ONE: RED/GREEN/WHITE

Warp
8/2 Cotton Clouds Aurora Earth
- Dark Red: 72 ends plus 2 floating selvedges = 74 ends, 230 yards (210.3 m)
- White: 120 ends, 375 yards (342.9 m)
- Kelly Green: 60 ends, 200 yards (182.9 m)

Weft
8/2 Cotton Clouds Aurora Earth
- Dark Red: 200 yards (182.9 m)
- White: 350 yards (320 m)
- Kelly Green: 200 yards (182.9 m)

Sparklers

Full Motif
24 ends

Sparklers Threading
Full Motif: 12 times
Partial Motif: 1 time

Partial Motif
12 ends

Tie-up and Treadling

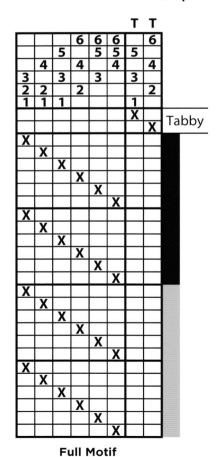

Tabby

Full Motif

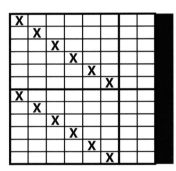

Partial Motif

Sparklers Treadling
Full Motif: 19 times
Partial Motif: 1 time

Sparklers Plus One

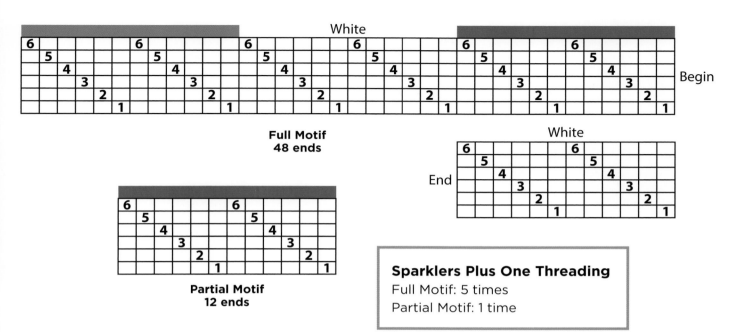

Full Motif
48 ends

Partial Motif
12 ends

White

Begin

End

Tie-up and Treadling

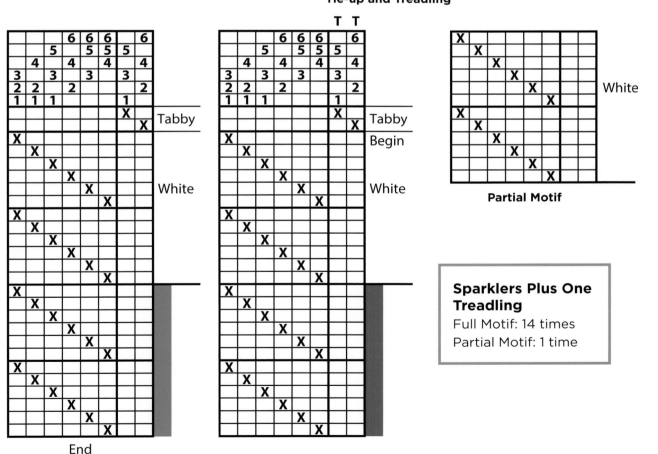

Tabby

White

End

Tabby

Begin

White

White

Partial Motif

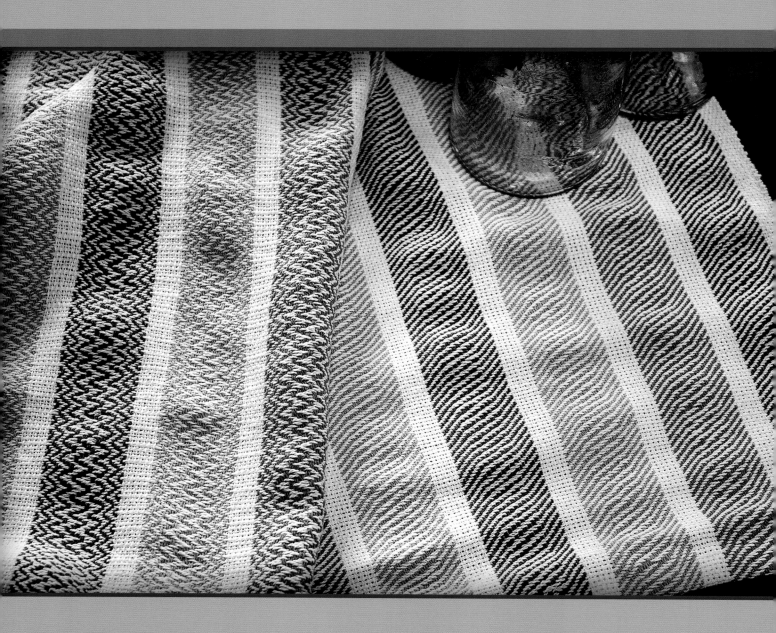

Galway Green

Many years ago, we made a trip to Ireland. It is still one of our favorite places that we have visited. Ireland has the reputation of being ever so green, and I can tell you that it is well earned. Since it rains almost every day, the fields display a vast array of different greens. This set of towels is an homage to that nation.

I used three different greens in the warp separated by white. The green sequence is as follows:

White	Green	White	Mill Gr	White	Nile Gr	White	Green	White	Nile Gr	White	Mill Gr	White	Green	White
10 ends	32 ends	10 ends	32 ends	10 ends	32 ends	10 ends	32 ends	10 ends	32 ends	10 ends	32 ends	10 ends	32 ends	10 ends

There are two different treadling patterns. You can weave one of each or just pick your favorite. Don't be surprised that you get some undulation when weaving these towels. This effect will straighten out as you weave. Also, the warp threads will pack in tighter because of the double threads in the threading. For this reason, you will have a higher ppi.

Weave your towel to 28 inches (71.1 cm) and weave four passes of a high-contrast color to separate the towels. Then weave your second towel. Finish your towels with a rolled hem.

Dimensions: 15 inches × 24.5 inches (38.1 × 62.2 cm)

Warp
Sett: 20 epi, 10 dent reed, 2 threads per dent
Length: 3-yard (2.7-m) warp
Threads: 10/2 Cotton Clouds Aurora Earth
- Green: 96 ends, 300 yards (274.3 m)
- Mill Green: 64 ends, 200 yards (182.9 m)
- Nile Green: 64 ends, 200 yards (182.9 m)
- White: 80 ends plus 2 floating selvedges = 82 ends, 275 yards (251.5 m)

Weft
10/2 Cotton Clouds Aurora Earth, White: 700 yards (640.1 m)

Threading

Alternate Motifs A and B:
  7 times
Motif A: 1 time
Follow the color sequence as indicated in the text on page 173.

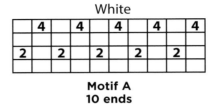

White

**Motif A
10 ends**

Color

**Motif B
32 ends**

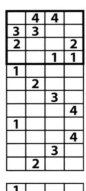

Treadling 1

Treadling 2

Treadling

Follow instructions in text on page 173.

All about Cats

These are the perfect towels for cat lovers! I'll admit, I somewhat lost control and kept coming up with different ideas. I just had to share them all. I'm sure you can think of more!

Black Cats

In the warp, the Borders and Motif B will be Black cotton. Motif A will be White cotton. For the black cats, you will be using 8/4 cotton. The horizontal stripes will be 8/2 Black, and the rest of the weft and tabby will be 8/2 White.

Multicolor Cats

In the warp, the Borders and Motif B will be Black cotton. Motif A will be White cotton. For the cats, you will be using double strands of 8/2 cotton in the indicated colors. The horizontal stripes will be 8/2 Black, and the rest of the weft and tabby will be 8/2 White.

Halloween Cats

In the warp, the Borders and Motif B will be Black cotton. Motif A will alternate using Dark Orange and Light Orange. You will have four Dark Orange warp stripes and three Light Orange stripes. The horizontal stripes will be 8/2 Black. Alternate using the Dark Orange and Light Orange in the individual blocks and tabby. For the cats, you will use 8/4 Black cotton. If using the different oranges is too confusing, use just the Dark Orange for your towels.

White Cats

In the warp, the Borders and Motif B will be White cotton. Motif A will be Kelly Green. For the cats, you will be using 8/4 cotton. The horizontal stripes are 8/2 White, and the rest of the weft and tabby are 8/2 Kelly Green.

All Cats (Treadling)

Begin each towel with 2 inches (5.1 cm) of plain weave. Then weave one horizontal stripe made of four passes. Weave four passes of plain weave, color determined by the towel you are creating, and then weave one cat repeat. Follow this step with another four passes of plain weave. Repeat this process until you have woven six rows of cats. End with one more horizontal stripe and 2 inches (5.1 cm) of plain weave. Weave four passes of a high-contrast color to separate the towels, and then weave your second towel, repeating the process. Finish your towels with a rolled hem.

I hope you have as much fun weaving these towels as I did creating the pattern. You could also make some wonderful table runners with this pattern. Enjoy!

Dimensions: 15 inches × 23 inches (38.1 × 58.4 cm)
Sett: 20 epi, 10 dent reed, 2 threads per dent
Length: 3-yard (2.7-m) warp

BLACK CATS

Warp

8/2 Cotton Clouds Aurora Earth
• Black: 48 ends plus 2 floating selvedges = 50 ends, 175 yards (160 m)
• White: 252 ends, 800 yards (731.5 m)

Weft

8/2 Cotton Clouds Aurora Earth
• White: 500 yards (457.2 m)
• Black: 35 yards (32 m)
Pattern thread (for cats): 8/4 cotton, Black: 150 yards (137.2 m)

MULTICOLOR CATS

Warp

8/2 Cotton Clouds Aurora Earth
• Black: 48 ends plus 2 floating selvedges = 50 ends, 175 yards (160 m)
• White: 252 ends, 800 yards (731.5 m)

Weft

8/2 Cotton Clouds Aurora Earth
• White: 500 yards (457.2 m)
• Black: 35 yards (32 m)
Pattern thread (for cats): 8/2 Cotton Clouds Aurora Earth—doubled
• Light Brown: 60 yards (54.9 m)
• Rust: 60 yards (54.9 m)
• Black: 60 yards (54.9 m)
• Chocolate: 60 yards (54.9 m)
• Cinnamon: 60 yards (54.9 m)

HALLOWEEN CATS

Warp

8/2 Cotton Clouds Aurora Earth
• Black: 48 ends plus 2 floating selvedges = 50 ends, 175 yards (160 m)
• Dark Orange: 144 ends, 450 yards (411.5 m)
• Light Orange: 108 ends, 340 yards (310.9 m)

Weft

8/2 Cotton Clouds Aurora Earth
• Dark Orange: 250 yards (228.6 m)
• Light Orange: 250 yards (228.6 m)
• Black: 35 yards (32 m)
Pattern thread (for cats): 8/4 Cotton by Cotton Clouds, Black: 150 yards (137.2 m)

WHITE CATS

Warp

8/2 Cotton Clouds Aurora Earth
• White: 48 ends plus 2 floating selvedges = 50 ends, 175 yards (160 m)
• Kelly Green: 252 ends, 800 yards (731.5 m)

Weft

8/2 Cotton Clouds Aurora Earth
• Kelly Green: 500 yards (457.2 m)
• White: 35 yards (32 m)
Pattern thread (for cats): 8/4 cotton, White: 150 yards (137.2 m)

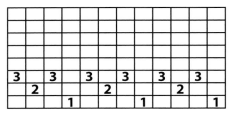

Threading
Border: 1 time
Alternate Motifs A and B:
  6 times
Motif A: 1 time
Border: 1 time

Border
12 ends

Motif A
36 ends

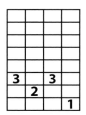

Motif B
4 ends

Tie-up and Treadling

T T

Tail—bottom of cat

Ears—top of cat

Treadling
1 full repeat is 1 cat.
Add tabby after
each pattern thread.
Follow instructions in
text on page 175.

Color Gamp Towels

These towels are fun to use but also serve another purpose! They allow you to see the interaction of two colors in both plain weave and twill. So, why is this important? Think of all the times you have been planning a project and wondered about color. Or maybe you have already started weaving and discovered that you didn't like your choices. It happens! I have multiple color gamps in a variety of threads, colors, and weave structures that I can refer to when designing. These gamps help me make suitable color choices.

For your towels, choose 10 colors that you like or use a lot. It makes no difference how they are arranged, but I keep color families together. Each stripe is 30 threads, which is 1.5 inches (3.8 cm) wide. Since I wanted only one repeat of each color in the weft, each block was woven 2.5 inches (6.4 cm), except for the first and last blocks, which were woven 3.5 inches (8.9 m) to allow for the rolled hem. I started with an outside color for the first block and worked across in order. Again, it makes no difference which color you start with.

Weave your first towel in tabby/plain weave. Then apply four passes of a high-contrast color to separate the towels. Weave your second towel in twill. Finish your towels with a rolled hem.

Dimensions: 15 inches × 24.5 inches (38.1 × 62.2 cm)

Warp

Sett: 20 epi, 10 dent reed, 2 threads per dent

Length: 3-yard (2.7-m) warp

Threads: 8/2 Cotton Clouds Aurora Earth

- Nassau Blue: 30 ends plus 1 floating selvedge = 31 ends, 100 yards (91.4 m)
- Baby Blue: 30 ends, 100 yards (91.4 m)
- Purple: 30 ends, 100 yards (91.4 m)
- Lavender: 30 ends, 100 yards (91.4 m)
- Kelly Green: 30 ends, 100 yards (91.4 m)
- Nile Green: 30 ends, 100 yards (91.4 m)
- Dark Red: 30 ends, 100 yards (91.4 m)
- Special Pink: 30 ends, 100 yards (91.4 m)
- Orange: 30 ends, 100 yards (91.4 m)
- Maize: 30 ends plus 1 floating selvedge = 31 ends, 100 yards (91.4 m)

Weft

8/2 Cotton Clouds Aurora Earth

- Nassau Blue: 50 yards (45.7 m)
- Baby Blue: 50 yards (45.7 m)
- Purple: 50 yards (45.7 m)
- Lavender: 50 yards (45.7 m)
- Kelly Green: 50 yards (45.7 m)
- Nile Green: 50 yards (45.7 m)
- Dark Red: 50 yards (45.7 m)
- Special Pink: 50 yards (45.7 m)
- Orange: 50 yards (45.7 m)
- Maize: 50 yards (45.7 m)

Threading

Threading
Motif: 75 times

4			
	3		
		2	
			1

**Threading
4 ends**

Tie-up and Treadling

				T	T
		4	4		4
	3	3		3	
2	2				2
1			1	1	

Twill treadling

X					
	X				
		X			
			X		

Tabby treadling

				X	
					X
				X	
					X

Treadling
See instructions in text on page 179.

Waste Not Want Not

How fun are these towels? In the evening when I watch television, I will often sit and tie thread pieces together—leftover loom waste that I just can't bear to throw away. These threads are every color imaginable. And because I do a lot of weaving, I have a lot of loom waste. These pieces are generally 8–10 inches (20.3–25.4 cm) long. If they are longer, I will cut them; otherwise, I'll have horizontal stripes. If I am working with 10/2 or 8/2 scraps, I will tie two of them together just so it goes a bit faster. These thrum balls are beautiful just to look at, so you could leave them in a basket for display. But I decided to use the thrum balls as weft thread. I did not trim the knots close but left the ends long. After multiple washings, those long pieces tend to disappear. You will notice that I separated the whites and neutrals into separate balls. That was my choice, but you certainly can blend them in with the colors.

Now for the warp! We all have those partial cones with a small amount of yardage. The photo above shows just a small sampling of what is in my stash. We can't really mix them with a new cone, since dye lots can vary and the difference could be very obvious. So, what to do? Make a multicolor warp! I didn't want to have obvious stripes, so I wound two colors and then changed out one and kept winding. It was a bit slower, but I got the look I wanted.

Then to the weaving! I used the white for some towels, the neutral for some, and finally the multicolor balls for the rest. Each towel has its own unique look.

The yardage required for these towels depends on how many you want to weave. If you have a McMorran balance, you can estimate the yardage you have in those little bits, but that really isn't necessary. For two 15-inch (38.1-cm) wide towels, sett at 20 epi and a 3-yard (2.7-m) warp, you will need approximately 900 yards (823 m). Add 30 inches (76.2 cm) for each additional towel. This is a generous warp. These towels are woven in plain weave. I experimented with a twill weave structure but found that it did not show well and was not worth all the extra effort. Begin your towel with 1.5 inches (3.8 cm) of plain weave in any color. Use up another small amount! Next, weave 26 inches (66 cm) of the towel with a thrum ball and then another 1.5 inches (3.8 cm) of plain weave. Put in four passes of a high-contrast color to separate your towels and repeat the process for each towel. Finish your towels with a rolled hem. I hope this project inspires you to use those little bits in a fun way.

Dimensions: 15 inches × 24 inches (38.1 × 61 cm)

Warp
Sett: 20 epi, 10 dent reed, 2 threads per dent
Length: 3-yard (2.7-m) warp
Threads: 8/2 Cotton Clouds Aurora Earth, multiple colors: 300 ends, 900 yards (823 m) total (2 towels)

Weft
Thrum balls
8/2 cotton in any color for plain weave at beginning and end—use any color that you want! Use up those small bits!

Threading
Motif: 75 times

**Motif
4 ends**

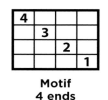

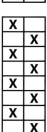

**Tie-up and
Treadling**

RESOURCES

Books

A Handweaver's Pattern Book by Marguerite P. Davison. Publisher: Marguerite P. Davison, Swarthmore, Pennsylvania.

A Weaver's Book of 8-Shaft Patterns by Carol Strickler. Interweave Press: Loveland, Colorado.

Learning to Weave by Deborah Chandler. Interweave Press: Loveland, Colorado.

The Handweaver's Pattern Directory by Anne Dixon. Interweave Press: Loveland, Colorado.

Online

Cottonclouds.com (Cotton Clouds threads)

Fabulousyarn.com

Handweaving.net (weaving drafts, tools, and documents)

Organiccottonplus.com

Tim's Treadle Reducer: https://www.cs.earlham.edu/~timm/treadle/

Other

Tom Knisely, instructor at Red Stone Glen Fiber Arts Center, York Haven, Pennsylvania

ACKNOWLEDGMENTS

This book has been a joy to create. So many towels and so many ideas! I was sure I wouldn't be able to design so many different towels. Instead, I have many more ideas and could fill this book two times over.

Special thanks to my husband, Dave, who learned to weave and then wove some of the towels in this book. He is very patient, and his work is meticulous. He also put up with me on those nights when I couldn't sleep because I had so many ideas rushing through my head.

Thank you to Jodi Ybarra of Cotton Clouds. When I needed to order fiber, she had it in the mail that day.

Thanks to Valynn Boy, who wove two sets of towels since I had loom limitations at the time. Thanks to my good friend Francie Appleman, who goes through the files and checks the math and charts for me. And my mentor Tom Knisely! He has always encouraged me in everything. I can never thank him enough. I also want to thank Stackpole Books and Candi Derr for their confidence in my work. I love you all!

Susan Kesler-Simpson

VISUAL INDEX

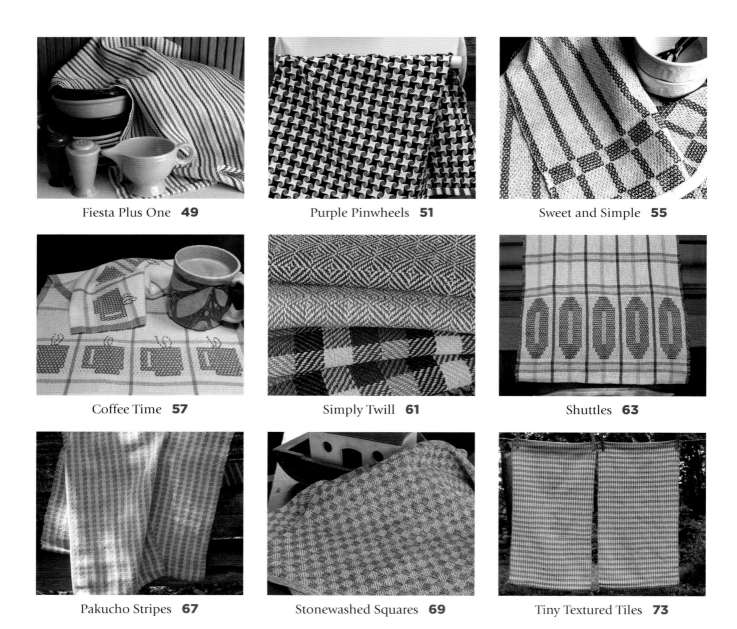

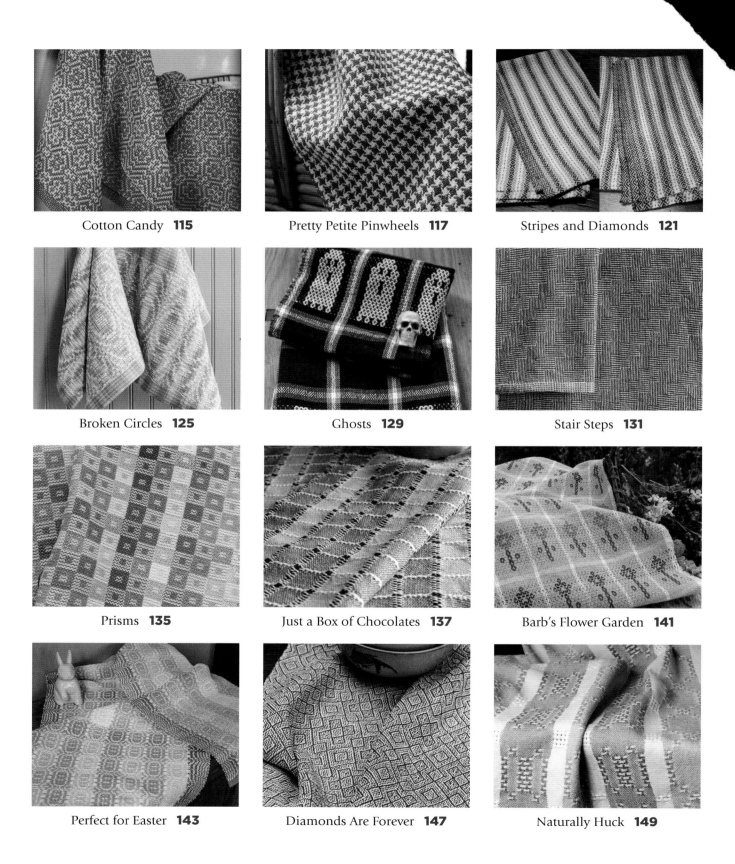

Beautiful Borders **153**

I Have a Heart for You **157**

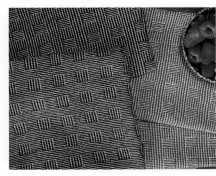

Razzleberry **159**

Diamonds and Lace **163**

Trio of Towels **165**

Sparklers Plus One **169**

Galway Green **173**

All about Cats **175**

Color Gamp Towels **179**

Waste Not Want Not **183**

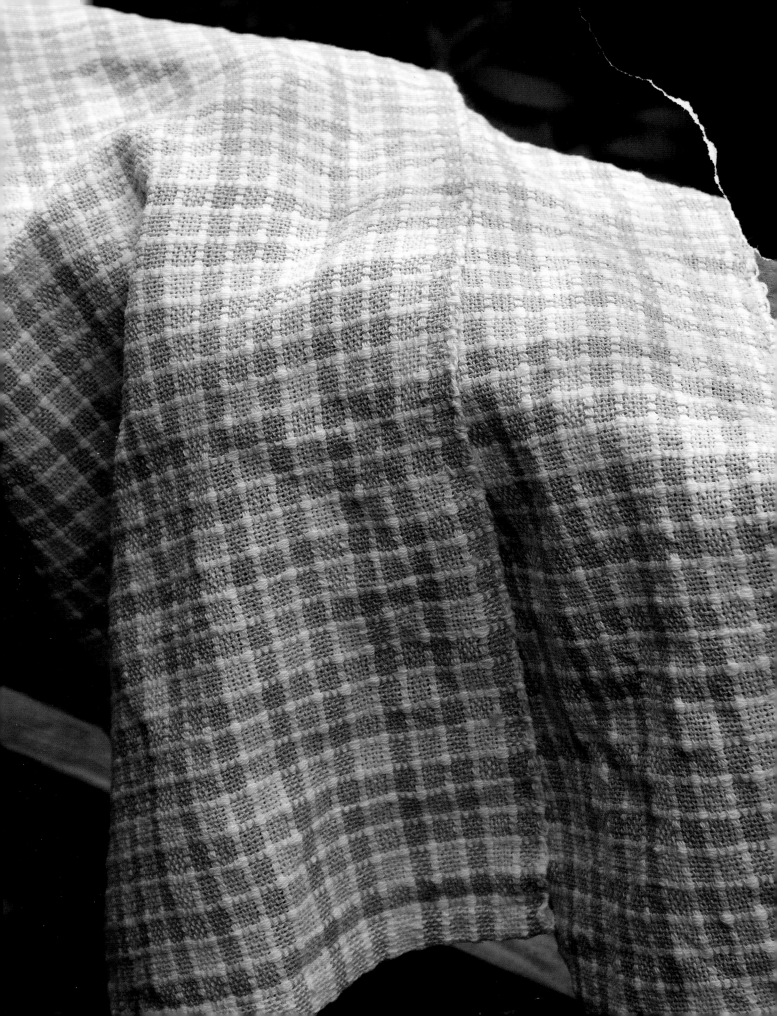